THE RESURRECTION AND THE AFTERLIFE

Compiled and Translated by

THE RESURRECTION AND THE AFTERLIFE

Compiled and Translated by

Ali Ünal

New Jersey

First published by Kaynak 1998

26 25 24 23   3 4 5 6

Published by Tughra Books
345 Clifton Ave.,
Clifton, NJ, 07011, USA

www.tughrabooks.com

Library of Congress Cataloging-in-Publication Data Available

Ünal, Ali
    Resurrection and the afterlife / Ali Ünal.
    p. cm.
    Includes bibliographical references and index.
    ISBN 0-9704370-0-5
1. Eschatology, Islamic. 2. Resurrection (Islam).
    3. Future life (Islam). 4. Islam--Doctrines I. Title.
    BP166.8 G85 2000
    297.2'3--dc21
00-010950

CONTENTS

FOREWORD

The topics of the resurrection and the afterlife always have generated a great deal of speculation. People want to know when it will occur, how it will be done, how it will affect them, and whether such things really will happen or not.

How we view these two topics affects how we live our lives. We want to know why we were created. We understand from our daily lives that nothing can exist without a purpose (even if we do not know what it is). Since we exist, we must have some purpose. But what is it? How can we discover it? And once we discover it, what should we do?

While asking such questions, others come up: Why is there so much injustice in the world? Why do dictators and tyrants enjoy themselves while the innocent suffer under their boots? Why do some people revel in luxury while others die from a lack of food or medicine? Where is the justice? Is God deaf? Did He leave after setting everything in motion? Is He no longer interested in us? Does He even exist?

On a less abstract level, our acceptance or rejection of the resurrection and the afterlife affect how we conduct our daily lives. If there is no judgment and resurrection, what is the point in being honest, nice to others, concerned with others' welfare, and trying to live an upright life? Without judgment there can be no reward or punishment, and so the most reasonable decision would be to make the most of our lives here and look out for ourselves. Why should we worry about eternal consequences when there are none?

But what about our loved ones and friends who have died? Will we ever see them again, or have they passed into eternal annihilation? How can children be consoled if one of their parents dies? How can elderly people be consoled while watching their family members and friends die one by one? How can our societies function if everyone is out for his or her own enjoyment, indulging their material and lustful needs without a thought for anyone else, and worrying only about themselves? Without belief in the resurrection and the afterlife, how can we survive?

But if there is a resurrection and a judgment, we have to look at the world in a totally different way. We must prepare ourselves for that day by doing what the Qur'an and the Prophet tell us to do: do good deeds, help and care about others, fight injustice and oppression, bring the carnal self under control, and seek to fulfill our obligations to God Almighty. People will control themselves and help others, which results in social peace and cooperation. People will no longer be sad when their loved ones die, for they know that they will see them in the eternal hereafter. And, because they have learned why they were created and what is expected of them, their minds and souls will be at rest, which allows them to live happy and productive lives dedicated to worshipping God and helping their fellow human beings.

Ali Ünal, basing himself on the Qur'an and Said Nursi's *Risale-i Nur*, explains such topics and answers many other questions related to the resurrection and the afterlife. In short, he relates that the Qur'an says life is a test for humanity. We are here to prepare ourselves for our future—and eternal—life either in Paradise or Hell. The definitions of "good" and "bad," "allowed" and "forbidden," were made crystal clear by Prophet Muhammad's life—his words, actions, ideas, practices, and so on. Given this knowledge, we must decide what to do with it, for we where we will spend eternity depends upon our choice.

According to Islam, human life has no meaning without the resurrection. How can there be testing if the earned reward or punishment cannot be bestowed in its entirety? How can there be purpose if people are born, live, and die, and are not judged for their deeds? How can there be justice if everybody is treated in the same way? But as this temporary, material world cannot manifest God's rewards and punishments fully, as the temporary cannot contain the eternal, there must be another world in which these rewards and punishments can be manifested in their entirety. That other world is the Hereafter, which we can reach only by being resurrected and judged by God.

CHAPTER 1
THE MEANING OF EXISTENCE AND LIFE

THE MEANING OF EXISTENCE AND LIFE

Said Nursi, one of the greatest thinkers of the twentieth century, presents the following argument for God's Unity and Existence: There are two ways to explain how a seed germinates underground to grow into an elaborate plant or tree, and how a sperm [and egg] grows into a human being. First, each innumerable particle operative in the growth process individually knows its place, functions, and environment, as well as its relations with all of the organism's other particles, cells, and larger wholes. Second, One Who has that vast knowledge employs them in the growth process and the formation of all living or non-living entities.

The following scientific experiment, reported in *Discover* (20 August 1993), clarifies this significant argument:

> Overbeck and his co-workers at the Baylor College of Medicine in Houston were trying to practice some gene therapy techniques by seeing if they could convert albino mice into colored ones. The researcher injected a gene essential to the production of the pigment melanin into the single-cell embryo of an albino mouse. Later they bred that mouse's offspring, half of which carried the gene on one chromosome of a chromosome pair. Classic Mendelian genetics told them that roughly a quarter of the grandchildren should carry the gene on both chromosomes—should be 'homozygous', in the language of genetics—and should therefore be colored.

> But the mice never got a chance to acquire color. 'The first thing we noticed,' says Overbeck, "was that we were losing about 25% of the grandchildren within a week after they were born."

> The explanation: The melanin-related gene that his group injected into the albino mouse embryo had inserted itself into a completely unrelated gene. An unfamiliar stretch of DNA in the middle of a gene wrecks that gene's ability to get its message read. So in the mice, it seems whatever protein the gene coded for went unproduced, whatever function the protein had went undone, and the stomach, heart, liver, and spleen all wound up in the wrong place. Somehow, too, the kidneys and pancreas were damaged, and that damage is apparently what killed the mice.

Overbeck and his colleagues have already located the gene on a particular mouse chromosome and are now trying to pin down its structure. That will tell them something about the structure of the protein the gene encodes, how the protein works, and when and where it is produced as the gene gets 'expressed', or turned on, "Is the gene expressed everywhere, or just on the left side of the embryo or just on the right side?" Overbeck wonders, "And when does it get expressed?"

These questions will take Overbeck far from the gene-transfer experiment. "We think there are at least 100,000 genes," he points out, "so the chances of this happening were literally one in 100,000."

THERE IS NO TRIAL AND ERROR IN NATURE

It will take thousands of tests and thousands of mice's lives to carry out this experiment successfully. However, there is no trial and error in nature. Any tree seed lying under the soil, provided that it faces no impediment, germinates and becomes a tree. Likewise, a human embryo grows into a living, conscious being equipped with intellectual and spiritual faculties.

The human body is a miracle of symmetry and of asymmetry. Scientists know how an embryo develops in the womb to form such symmetry and asymmetry. What they do not know is how a particle, which reaches the embryo through the mother and functions as a building block to form the body, can distinguish between right and left, determine each organ's place, insert itself in the exact place of a certain organ, and understand the extremely complicated relations and requirements among cells and organs. This is so complicated a process that, for example, if a single particle meant for the right eye's pupil went to the ear, it could lead to malfunction or even death.

In addition, all animate beings are made from the same elements (soil, air, and water) and are similar to each other in their bodily members and organs. Yet they are almost completely different from each other in their bodily features, visage, character, desires, and ambitions. Each individual is so unique that he or she can be identified absolutely by his or her fingerprints.

How can we explain this? There can be no third alternative. Either each particle does this on its own, or else it is done by a Creator. However far back we go to ascribe this to cause and effect and heredity, these two alternatives remain valid.

This argument, frequently emphasized by Said Nursi, may lose its appeal when one objects: "Since everything takes place according to a certain program and the principle of cause and effect, why does a particle need to know all of this information?" However, such an objection means trying to find an explanation for existence from within existence, which is not acceptable, for it does not explain how the first creation took place.

THE UNIVERSE IS AN INSEPARABLE WHOLE

Materialistic science, whether biology or physics, reflects upon existence from within and is dazzled by the universe's apparent self-organization. Everything appears to happen according to certain principles and the law of cause and effect.

Materialistic science, which ascribes creativity to causality, is based on radical fragmentation. It considers nature a mechanism with no inherent value and meaning, and thus isolates an object by cutting off its connections with the rest of the world. If we look at the created world as it really is, not as we wish to see it, it becomes clear that the universe is an inseparable whole. All of its beings, on whatever level, are interrelated, interconnected, and interdependent, like concentric or intersecting circles. The discoveries of modern physics point toward this unity, an unbroken wholeness that denies the materialistic fragmentation of the world into separate and independent parts.

Quantum physics holds that every particle is linked to the rest of the universe and cannot be isolated from it. This oneness includes human beings. For this reason, a cause can produce an effect only if it can produce the whole universe in which that effect takes place, for that effect cannot exist without the whole universe. Whatever causes a flower's seed to exist must be responsible for the flower itself, as well as for the apparent causes of its existence: air, water, sunlight, and soil. Given their interdependence, whatever causes a flower to exist must be responsible for a tree. And, given their interrelation, whatever causes a tree to exist must be responsible for the forest, and so on.

Such interconnectedness means that all things in the universe, regardless of the distance separating them, help each other. This mutual helping is comprehensive. For example, air, water, fire, soil, the sun, the sky, and everything else help humanity in an extraordinarily prearranged manner. This is also true of the individual's bodily cells, members, and systems, all of which cooperate to keep him or her alive. Soil, air, water, heat, and underground bacteria cooperate to maintain plant life. This cooperation and mutual helping, observed among unconscious beings but displaying knowledge and conscious purpose, cannot be attributed to lifeless, blind, and ignorant causes.

In addition, the universe's splendid harmony, organization, and order require an all-encompassing knowledge, will, and power. To create a single atom and put it in its exact place requires an all-encompassing knowledge, will, and power that can create the whole cosmos. This is clearly beyond the ability of a cause that is blind, impotent, transient, and dependent, as well as devoid of knowledge, will, and power.

Moreover, what we call *causes* or the *law of causality* have only nominal existence. In other words, they have no external, material existence. If we ask those who attribute creation to causality or causes how a flower is created, they cannot respond that water, soil, and sunlight make it. They must explain how soil or water or sunlight know exactly what to do, how they do it, and what qualities they have that enable a flower to grow.

MATTER AND CHANCE

If we say that matter is the source or originator of existence, we have to accept that lifeless, blind, deaf, mute, and ignorant matter has an all-encompassing knowledge. Otherwise, how could it create such a perfectly functioning and interdependent universe? Is such a proposition so irrefutable that the existence of a Creator having an all-encompassing knowledge, will, and power can be denied?

According to the principles of classical physics and of new physics, matter is changeable and susceptible to external intervention. Thus it cannot be eternal or capable of origination. Also, can matter create beings and bestow them with characteristics that it does not possess, such as sentient life, knowledge, power, and consciousness?

Materialists, however, see things differently—they do not see different things. They ask us to believe that this cosmos, whose innate order and harmony they do not deny, is the work of chance, of chaos and disorder, of sheer accident. Then they ask us to believe that it is sustained by the mechanistic interplay of causes—which even they cannot determine or explain with certainty—that are themselves created, impotent, ignorant, transient, and purposeless. Somehow, through laws that appeared out of nowhere, such causes produced the orderly works of art of symphonies of harmony and equilibrium that surround us.

But just look at the universe's purposive arrangement, organization, and harmony. Can we seriously entertain the idea that all of it was caused by chance or coincidence? There are trillions of cells in a human body, each of which contains about one million proteins. The possibility of a protein occurring by chance are infinitesimally small. Without One Who has the power of choice to prefer its existence and the absolute power to create; Who has an absolute, all-comprehensive knowledge to prearrange its relations with other proteins, with the cell and all bodily parts, and place it just where it must be, a single protein cannot exist. The following experiment proves this point:

> Suppose you take ten pennies and mark them from 1 to 10. Put them in your pocket and give them a good shake. Now try to draw them out in sequence from 1 to 10, putting each coin back in your pocket after each draw. Your chance of drawing No. 1 is 1 in 10. Your chance of drawing 1 and 2 in succession would be 1 in 100. Your chance of drawing 1, 2, and 3 in succession would be 1 in 1,000. Your chance of drawing 1, 2, 3, and 4 in succession would be 1 in 10,000 and so on, until your chance of drawing from No. 1 to No. 10 in succession would reach the unbelievable figure of one chance in 10 billion.
>
> The object in dealing with so simple a problem is to show how enormously figures multiply against chance.
>
> So many essential conditions are necessary for life on our earth that it is mathematically impossible that all of them could exist in proper relationship by chance on any one earth at one time. Therefore, there must be in nature some form of intelligent direction. If this be true, then there must be a purpose.[1]

Attributing creative power to nature, natural laws, matter, or to such notions as chance and necessity, is a personal opinion that has nothing to do with an objective, scientific investigation. Similarly, denying the Creator is not an act of reason but an act of will. In short, such assertions are no more than attempts to distribute the Creator's properties among the created so that human beings can set themselves up as absolute owners and rulers of whatever they possess and are.

1　A. Cressy Morrison, *Man Does Not Stand Alone,* Fleming H. Revell Company, New York: 1945.

WHAT A FALLING STONE MEANS[2]

To have a clearer understanding of this issue, consider the law of general gravity, an undeniably established scientific fact. Observations and experiments have shown that any two objects attract each other or exert force upon each other in proportion to their masses and in inverse proportion to the square of the distance between them.

The force of attraction (gravity) operates in such events as a falling object and the Earth's revolving around the sun. Science presents gravity as if it were the cause of such events. However, gravity is only a concept used to explain those events. In other words, there is an attraction observed between objects. To explain this attraction, we give it a name (for example, the law or force of gravitation) and think that we have explained everything. We follow the same approach when dealing with all other things and "natural" events.

Scientists cannot explain the nature of gravity. Basing themselves on the assertion that they have explained many previously unknown events, they claim that they will be able to explain gravity and everything else in the future. Nevertheless, they cannot explain the real cause of all events in the universe. What they do is to establish the fact that a certain event will recur forever given the same conditions, and then make a generalization and call it a law. For example, after observing that an object thrown into the air will fall, they generalize that all objects thrown into the air will fall and then produce a mathematical formula to express this event.

Scientists work in the following manner. They calculate and state beforehand how long it will take an object thrown into the air, with a certain force and at a certain angle, to fall and how far away it will fall. Since the associated events apparently take place in a cause-and-effect series, knowing what effect or event will occur in the next step does not require understanding why it happens as it does. Therefore, we suppose that gravity will be understood as, say, dependent on an exchange between certain particles or the obliquity of spatial time.

But these scientific methods do not explain why such an exchange takes place, why spatial time becomes oblique, why that exchange or obliquity occurs according to certain mathematical formulations so that objects attract each other, why objects attract each other at all, or why this event of attraction

---

2 Salih Adem, "What a Falling Stone Means," *Islamic Perspectives on Science*, Kaynak, Izmir: 1998.

takes place according to a mathematical formula. Our familiarity with events taking place in nature causes us to ignore the fact that every thing and event in nature is a miracle. In order to see why gravity is a dazzling miracle, we should consider it more closely.

Consider a stone falling unhindered from certain height point. It will realize a certain trajectory due to gravity. It will move faster and faster and finally hit the ground. How the stone will accelerate, how long it will take it to reach the ground, and how it will move at every second of its trajectory depends on the stone's distance from the Earth's center, the Earth's mass, and gravity's constant. Thus, the stone does not move at random; each movement during its fall is calculable by mathematical formulas.

From this extremely regular movement, we conclude that if the stone were to fall by itself, without any agent directing or determining its trajectory, it must have accurate knowledge of gravity's constant, the Earth's mass, and its distance from the Earth's center at each moment of its trajectory. It then would fall in conformity with that knowledge. Can anyone seriously entertain such an absurd view? How could a stone, devoid of all intelligence, possibly calculate such a downward path?

In reality, this apparently simple event is so complex that everything in the universe that has a certain mass exerts some degree of attraction on the falling stone. As a result, the falling stone is influenced by all of them.[3]

To determine its trajectory, the stone must know the exact distance between itself and each of about 1,080 particles in the universe. It must calculate this distance accurately at each moment of its trajectory, as well as the attraction that each particle exerts upon it according to the mathematical formula of gravity (a force that changes every moment), and focus all those forces to a single point based on each one's direction. Needless to say, not even the most powerful supercomputer can accomplish such a feat. And yet some people think a stone can do so! The position of each particle with respect to the stone changes every moment during its fall. Thus, the simplest-seeming movement in the universe requires a comprehensive knowledge and mastery of an infinite number of interrelated processes.

---

3 Here we do not consider such other essential forces as the electromagnetic and nuclear ones, which have a determining effect on an object's movement. Expressed with certain mathematical formulas, these forces make an item's movement even more complex.

Since any event taking place in the universe is connected with each parti-cle in the universe, as well as with the universe itself, only one with perfect knowledge of each particle and the whole universe, who sees the whole uni-verse and each particle in it, can determine and direct all of the universe's movements. Also, since the law of gravity and all other operative physical laws are the same and uniform throughout the universe, the one who makes such laws operative must be an absolutely powerful one who dominates each item therein. Otherwise, each atom must have an eye seeing the whole universe simultaneously; know the position, mass, electrical charge—in short all the physical features—of each particle in the universe; and be aware of and obey all of its self-originated physical laws.

Every event and item in the universe is interrelated. Whatever takes place does so according to certain laws. Therefore, even the smallest, most insignifi-cant-seeming event cannot take place without one with an absolute, perfect knowledge of the universe and all its particles, as well as an absolute power governing it. Said Nursi expresses this fact as follows:

> If the existence and operation of the universe is not attributed to God Almighty; one must admit that each particle has the attributes of the Necessarily Existent Being, and that each particle should both dominate and be dominated by all other particles. Again, each particle should have an all-encompassing will and knowledge, for the existence of a single thing is dependent on all things, and one who does not own the universe cannot rule a single particle.

After explaining how complex a phenomenon gravitation is, what is its real cause? The relation sensed between a falling stone and the moon's rotation around the Earth in a fixed orbit led Newton to discover the law of gravity. Ever since this law was accepted, the cause of a falling object has unquestionably been accepted as gravity. However, it is not necessary that this movement's real cause be the force of the Earth's attraction or the existence of another material cause.

Consider this: Imagine that some animate beings live on a two-dimension-al table. They are aware only of this table, and have no knowledge about the three-dimensional world around them. Someone from the three-dimensional world shoots at the table according to a specific pattern, thereby making holes at equal distances from each other. Seeing this, the beings living on the table inevitably will conclude that each hole causes another one to be made. But as we know, they were caused by someone shooting from the outside world.

This is how scientists who attribute every thing and event to the law of causality view the working of the universe. Are nearby objects attracted to each other (for example, the attraction of a falling stone toward the ground) because of the objects themselves, or is there another source forcing the objects to such a movement?[4]

In short, an object moves according to the law of gravity, and thus each of its movements can be described mathematically. This requires as many masses and distances as exist in the universe, as well as the distances among them, to be known in their mutual, complex relations. Who can know such information other than One Who is All-Knowing? This One also must have an absolute will to choose and assign the appropriate law for each event. The uniformity of the law's operation throughout the universe calls for the unity of that All-Knowing and All-Willing One. The obedience of everything to those laws demonstrates that that One is also All-Powerful. The laws' invariability and stability, as well as the universe's magnificent, unchanging order and harmony, show that that One is Self-Subsistent and All-Subsisting.

Given all of this, a stone falls because of the existence of an All-Knowing, All-Willing, All-Powerful, Self-Subsistent, and All-Subsisting, Single One. No one or thing in the universe has the necessary knowledge, will, and power to cause a stone to fall. Every thing and event in the universe is too complex and magnificent to be engendered by any material cause. And so, humanity is left with one option: admit and recognize God's Existence and Unity.

CONCLUSION[5]

Causality leads to the vicious chain of cause and effect, for each cause is also an effect, and each effect is totally different from the cause. However, what scientists call things and effects are, in reality, so full of art and beneficial purposes that, let alone their simple immediate causes, even if all causes gathered together they would be unable to produce a single thing.

When we break this chain, the meaningless world of materialism gives way to a world illumined with meaning and purpose. The universe becomes

---

4   Attraction is the simplest event in the universe. What about a honeybee's ability to make honey or a cow's ability to give milk? These require far more complex physical interactions, chemical reactions, and cause and effect relationships.

5   Information taken mostly from Dr. Collin Turner, "Risale-i Nur: A Revolution of Belief," paper offered to a conference held about Bediüzzaman Said Nursi in Istanbul in 1993.

like a vast book addressing humanity, making known its Author. In this way, its readers can learn and increase their knowledge of their Maker, and strengthen their belief and certainty in the fundamentals of faith.

In the universe, beings come into existence as though from nowhere. Their order and mutual relationships and duties utterly refute all materialistic claims and atheistic reasoning. They affirm that they are nothing but the property and creatures of a Single Creator. Each rejects the false notions of chance and causality. Each ascribes all other beings to its own Creator. Each is a proof that the Creator has no partners. During their brief lives, and according to their own particular purpose, goal, and mission, each one acts only as a mirror to reflect various Divine Attributes and countless configurations of the Divine Names. For example, through their coming into life, impotence and contingence, their total dependence on factors other than themselves, all beings clearly demonstrate that they owe their existence to the One Who necessarily exists, creates, and has power over all things. Through their transience and death, they show that One's permanence.

The signs of God, as well as all things and events in the universe, serve as mirrors to reveal His Names and Attributes to us in new and ever-changing forms and configurations. Such a display is designed to elicit our acknowledgement, acceptance, submission, love, and worship. Therefore, becoming a true believer involves a process: contemplation to knowledge, knowledge to affirmation, affirmation to belief or conviction, and conviction to submission.

Since each new moment sees the revelation of fresh aspects of Divine truth, this process is continuous. A believer's external and formal acts of worship contribute to this process. As a result, belief is subject to increase or decrease, or becoming stronger or weaker, according to the process' continuance. The reality of belief deserves most of our attention. From this, the realities of Divine religion will follow inevitably.

The meaning of existence or life is not confined to the study of nature and understanding its origin. It also concentrates on humanity's ontological character. Each individual is born in total ignorance; the desire to know ourselves and our world is innate. Thus "Who am I? Where did I come from? What is this place? Why am I here? Who is responsible for creating me? What do life and death want from me?" These are questions that each person much answer, either through direct observation or blind acceptance of others' answers. How one lives and acts in this world is totally dependent upon how these questions are answered.

These questions are answered either by one's ego or Divine Revelation (manifested as Divine religions). History records the conflicts between these two answers. Ego rejects Revelation and claims self-ownership by appropriating for itself whatever its Creator gives it, and by attributing to itself all accomplishments that God Almighty confers on it. The result of such a view is human wretchedness and unhappiness. All it has produced so far is Pharaohs, Nimrods, Neros, and other tyrants, not to mention those who, embracing their carnal desires, have gone astray and misled others.

The other answer has resulted in Prophets, saints, and other examples of virtuousness. Its core is the individual's consciousness of servanthood, its power lies in acknowledging inherent weakness before God Almighty's absolute Power, and its wealth in admitting inherent poverty before His Riches. It also requires deep devotion and worship in absolute thankfulness, together with continuous reflection on His signs in the universe, and ongoing enthusiasm in preaching His religion. The Divine Religion is a guided tour of the cosmos and of each individual's inner world. The traveler seeking such answers along this path will find them.

The secular, self-consuming society brought about by scientific materialism and self-worship is designed to blind and conceal on all levels. It seeks to mask its failure to live up to its promises, and that the secular trinity of "unlimited progress, absolute freedom, and unrestricted happiness" is meaningless. Moreover, it seeks to cover up the fact that economic and scientific progress, the underlying ethos of which is secular humanism, has turned the modern world into a spiritual wasteland and ravaged generation after generation.

Yet some people are beginning to awake, to realize the illusion under which they have been living. The disease of ego must be pointed out to such people. One suffering from cancer cannot be cured by receiving a new coat. Not only the West is suffering from this disease, for its victims can be found all over the world. What is needed is a correct diagnosis, radical surgery, and constant follow-up treatment.

LIFE: ITS VALUE AND PURPOSES[6]

The perfection of a thing's existence is through life. Moreover, life is the real basis and light of existence. Consciousness, in turn, is the light of life. Life also

---

6 Information taken mostly from Said Nursi, *The Words*, The Light, Inc., 29th Word, New Jersey: 2005.

constitutes the foundation of everything and appropriates everything for each living thing. Only through life can a living creature claim that everything belongs to it. It can claim the world as its home, and the entire universe as its property conferred upon it by the Giver of Life.

Just as light causes (concrete) things to be seen and, according to one theory, is the real cause of color, so life may be said to unveil the creation. Life causes potentials to be realized and gives archetypes (the existence of things in the Creator's Knowledge) material existence. Through it, particularity acquires universality and universals are concentrated in particulars.

Life also causes existence to attain perfection and possess a soul by making countless factors unite to form a whole—a sentient, percipient being. Furthermore, life is the manifestation of oneness in the realm of multiplicity, the reflection of unity in plurality. See how lonely a substance is without life, even though it is as big as a mountain. Its interactions are restricted to its own location. Being unconscious of other existents, nothing in the universe can mean anything to it. Then consider a small creation: the honeybee. Due to its close interactions with the universe, particularly with plants and flowers, it can view the Earth as the garden or market in which it conducts its business. Through its unconscious "instinctive" senses, which enthuse and motivate it, as well as its external and inner senses, the honeybee has close relations and familiarity with most species in the world.

If the effect of life on a lowly honeybee is so great, how much greater will it be on a human being who actively expands his or her consciousness, reason, and intellect. A human being, through his or her reason and consciousness (the lights of life), travels through the higher corporeal and spiritual worlds as easily as going from one room to another. That is, just as a conscious and living being may go in spirit to those worlds, those worlds can come to a person's mirror-like spirit by being reflected there.

Life is the greatest evidence of God's Unity and source of His bounty, a most subtle manifestation of His Compassion, and a most hidden and delicate embroidery of His art. Life is so mysterious and subtle that even the life of plants, the simplest level of life, and the awakening of a seed's life-force at the beginning of a plant's life, is still not understood fully. Although such an event is considered common, it has remained a mystery from the time of Adam, for the human mind remains unable to grasp the nature of life.

Life, in both its outer or material and inner or immaterial aspects, is pure. The Divine Power creates life directly without the participation of causes, while it employs natural causes to create everything else. God creates everything but life behind the veil of natural causes so that human beings, being unable to discern Divine Wisdom in some events, do not attribute to Him that which they consider unpleasant.

LIFE IN THE WORDS OF A SCIENTIST

A. C. Morrison writes:

> Life is a sculptor and shapes all living things; an artist that designs every leaf of every tree, that colors the flowers, the apple, the forest, and the plumage of the bird of paradise. Life is a musician and has taught each bird to sing its love songs, the insects to call each other in the music of their multitudinous sounds.

> Life has given to man alone mastery over combined sound vibrations and has furnished the material for their production.

> Life is an engineer, for it has designed the legs of the grasshopper and the flea, the coordinated muscles, levers and joints, the tireless beating heart, the system of electric nerves of every animal, and the complete system of circulation of every living thing.

> Life is a chemist that gives taste to our fruits and spices and perfume to the rose. Life synthesizes new substances which Nature has not yet provided to balance its processes and to destroy invading life... Life's chemistry is sublime, for not only does it set the rays of the sun to work to change water and carbonic acid into wood and sugar, but, in doing so, releases oxygen that animals may have the breath of life.

> Life is a historian, for it has written its history page by page, through the ages, leaving its record in the rocks, an autobiography which only awaits correct interpretation.

> Life protects its creations by the abundance of food in the egg and prepares many of its infants for active life after birth, or by conscious motherhood stores food in preparation for her young. Life produces life-giving milk to meet immediate needs, foreseeing this necessity and preparing for events to come.

> Matter has never done more than its laws decree. The atoms and molecules obey the dictates of chemical affinity, the force of gravity, the

influences of temperature and electric impulses. Matter has no initiative, but life brings into being marvelous new designs and structures.

What life is no man has yet fathomed; it has no weight or dimensions... Nature did not create life; fire-blistered rocks and a saltless sea did not meet the necessary requirements. Gravity is a property of matter; electricity we now believe to be matter itself; the rays of the sun and stars can be deflected by gravity and seem to be akin to it. Man is learning the dimensions of the atom and is measuring its locked-up power, but life is illusive, like space. WHY?

Life is fundamental and is the only means by which matter can attain understanding. Life is the only source of consciousness and it alone makes possible knowledge of the works of God which we, still half blind, yet know to be good.[7]

THE VALUE OF HUMAN LIFE AND ITS PURPOSES[8]

A visible but oft-neglected difference between human and other types of life is instructive here. On Earth, four classes of beings work for and serve great, comprehensive purposes:

• *Inanimate objects, including subatomic particles, atoms, molecules and elements.* All living beings are made from these objects. They serve universal purposes in a complicated, amazing way, but do not know what they do or why they do it.

• *Plants.* They have some degree of life and serve animals and human beings as food. Also, addressing themselves to their senses by displaying spectacular scenes, spreading pleasant scents, and playing the most touching kind of music, they satisfy human senses (in particular, those of seeing, smelling and hearing) and decorate the Earth. However, they do not know what kind of universal purposes they serve or what significant results they yield.

• *Animals.* They perform tasks based on their abilities. Although they do not know why they are doing what they do, they derive some sort of pleasure from their work. A sheep, for example, gives milk, wool, and meat; a dog is a loyal friend; and birds are the loveliest singers in gardens or mountains.

---

7 A. Cressy Morrison, *Man Does Not Stand Alone*, 31-36.
8 Said Nursi, *The Words*, The Light, Inc., 29th Word, New Jersey: 2005.

- *Humanity.* Only human beings are conscious. They know what they are doing, why and for whom they are doing it, and why everybody else is working. People also can supervise and employ other people for their own advantage. However, human beings did not create themselves. Although of the same elements and living on the same substances, each individual is unique in countenance and character. Thus, each individual can be identified correctly by even his or her fingerprints.

People have no part in determining their physical features, family, race, color, birth date or place, and even their own nature. Their free will also is limited. For example, their role in producing bread is insignificant when compared with that of the One Who organizes the sun, rain, and soil; a wheat seed's germination, growth, and life; the seasons; and the mutual helping between these elements.

Besides, people did not establish the basic conditions of life—they cannot prevent hunger, thirst, and sleep. They have no authority over the cycle of day and night or their bodies; they function automatically. For example, if they had to "wind" their hearts at exactly the same hour every morning like a clock to continue living, they would certainly have forgotten to do so every day.

Another interesting fact is that from the very moment an animal is born, it seems to know what to do. As if trained in another realm, it comes (or rather is sent) into the world and acquires full possession of those functions and abilities that it needs to survive within several hours, days, or months. For example, a sparrow or a bee acquires (or rather is inspired with), in less than a month, the ability to integrate into its environment in a way that would take an individual many years.

This reveals an important fact: Animals have no obligation or responsibility to seek perfection through learning, progress through scientific knowledge, or pursue prayer and supplication by displaying their impotence. They are obliged only to act within the bounds of their innate faculties, which is the mode of worship specified for them.

In contrast, people are born completely ignorant of life and their environment; we need to learn everything. Acquiring such knowledge requires our whole lifetime. We appear to have been sent here in such a state of weakness and inability that it takes us as long as 2 years even to learn how to walk; maybe 15 years to learn how to distinguish between good and evil. By living in a society, we eventually learn how to choose between what is beneficial and harmful.

Despite these basic differences, human life is the most valuable, for whatever exists was created to produce humanity. We are the fruit of the tree of creation. Just as a tree is grown for the sake of its fruit and its whole life is directed to yield this fruit, the whole universe serves humanity. Thus, each human being has the same value as the entire universe.

One might even say that its value is greater than the universe, for each individual is equipped with consciousness and other intellectual faculties that make it superior to all other life forms. In one instant, the human imagination can travel throughout and far beyond the universe. We can speak; experience very complicated feelings, desires, and goals; as well as learn, think, judge, reason, and employ other living beings. Therefore, our value lies not in our physical composition and material aspect, but in the metaphysical dimension of life.

The Hand of Power that created humanity made a great "expenditure" on each human being by attaching the greatest value to them. That is, in addition to their mental and spiritual faculties that no worldly scales can weigh, it included in their physical or biological composition almost all elements of the tree of creation. Each individual's physical or biological composition is so marvelous and expensive that if humanity joined together and built factories to produce a single cell, they would fail. When we consider only the neurons' structure and tasks and the thousands of cords extending from the brain to each of the more than trillions of cells in a human body, we can get a glimpse of what an amazing and miraculous creation we really are.

Despite this miraculous mechanism and the expenditure made on it, our earthly life is very short. Many people die soon after birth. However, the cost for and value of each individual, regardless of how long he or she lives, is the same. So short a life, despite such a vast expenditure and having the same essential value as a long one, cannot have been made for the life itself. Nor can it be limited to this world. It must have far-reaching aims, and there must be ways to eternalize it.

THE NATURE AND AIMS OF HUMAN LIFE

As the universe witnesses, everything reflects God in one way or another. For example, all beauty in creation is but a dim manifestation of God's absolute Beauty, for nothing can make itself beautiful. In addition, all beauty in the universe is defective, fleeting, and decaying, as this is the nature of created things.

This demonstrates that a thing's beauty does not belong to itself; rather, it belongs to an All-Beautiful One.

It also demonstrates that the One Who is All-Beautiful is one, unique and peerless, for He has no defects. By making everything beautiful, He shows that He is Beautiful. By assigning each thing or being an imperfect, particular beauty, He shows that He is One and peerless, and has an absolute, perfect Beauty. Likewise, beings demonstrate through their creation that God is the All-Living and Giver of Life, and that He is Eternal through their death.

Consider this: When you stand by a river, you see countless images of the sun reflected in floating bubbles. When those bubbles enter a tunnel, the images disappear. However, other bubbles coming into your field of vision will show the same reflections. When they enter the tunnel, the images also will disappear. This shows that those images do not belong to the bubbles; rather, by reflecting its image, they show the sun's existence. Through their disappearance, they demonstrate their transience vis-à-vis the sun's permanence.

Human beings are the same. Through their creation, impotence and contingence, as well as their total dependence on factors other than themselves, human beings demonstrate that they owe their existence to the One Who necessarily exists, creates, and has power over all things. Through their transience and death and being recruited by new ones, they show the permanence of that One.

So, whatever exists and happens is a result of God's manifesting His relevant Names. All of His Names manifested in the universe are localized in a human being. We hear because God is All-Hearing and has given us the ability to hear. We see, speak, move, and can learn and reason because God is All-Seeing, All-Speaking, All-Acting, and All-Knowing. However, as our bodies and very nature cannot receive the complete manifestation of any Divine Name, all of our powers and faculties are defective. And, because we are not eternal, since each of us has a beginning and an end, we are not absolute and permanent.

Thus, human life is an index of wonders originating in the Divine Names. It is a measure to consider the Divine Attributes and Perfections, a unit to know the "worlds" in the universe, a catalogue of the macrocosm, a map of the universe and its fruit or compressed form, and a set of keys with which to open the Divine Power's hidden treasuries. Human life is an inscribed word, a wisdom-displaying word written by the Pen of Power. Observed and sensed, it points to the Divine Beautiful Names.

Human life is a mirror to reflect the Divine manifestation of Divine Oneness and as the Eternally-Besought-of-All. Through its comprehensive nature as the focal point for all the Divine Names manifested in the world, it functions as a mirror to the Single and Eternally-Besought One. Its perfection lies in knowing and believing in God, and then loving Him and His creatures because of Him. We are expected to establish the reflection of God's Light, comprising all His Attributes and Names just as the sun's light comprises its seven colors, in the center of our hearts. This is why, as the meaning of a hadith *qudsi* says, while expressing a believer's rank among creatures: "(God said): I am not contained in the heavens and Earth; I am contained in the believer's heart."

Being an index of the manifestations of Divine Names and Attributes, and having a heart "containing" the Creator has the following implications. In addition to functioning "naturally" as a mirror to reflect Divine acts, Names, and Attributes, we should consciously weigh the bounties conferred by Absolute Mercy on the scales of the senses established in our bodies. After doing this, we should offer thanks on their bodies' behalf.

By acting like God, meaning that we follow His command to the best of our ability, we must be a "conscious mirror" that reflects His Grace, Beauty, Mercy, Forgiveness, Generosity, Justice, and so on. This is how believers proclaim their worship and servanthood to the Court of the Master in terms of speech, action, and the tongue of their nature or disposition.

In conclusion: A great expenditure has been made on human life so that it will become a mirror in which God's Names and Attributes are reflected. Such a function cannot be limited to this short, fleeting world; rather, it requires that humanity be sent to an eternal world. Although our lives bear certain fruit in this world, we will receive its full return in another, everlasting world. As we are so valuable in the sight of the Creator, Who created us as the index of all creation and its best pattern, we cannot pass into non-existence by death. Otherwise, such great expenditure and value would go to waste and be futile. Such an event is impossible, for the universe contains nothing futile—God does not involve Himself in anything futile and wasteful.

Given this, it is not right or reasonable for people to waste their lives by gratifying fleeting carnal desires and seeking transient worldly pleasures. Life should be spent in the quest to realize the purposes assigned to it by its Giver.

CHAPTER 2
BENEFITS OF BELIEF IN THE RESURRECTION AND THE AFTERLIFE

BENEFITS OF BELIEF IN THE
RESURRECTION AND THE AFTERLIFE[9]

Materialism was born in Europe in the middle of the eighteenth century. The British philosopher George Berkeley first used this term to mean an unjustified confidence in matter's existence. Later on, it was used to signify a philosophical movement or school attributing the origin of existence to matter and denying the existence of anything immaterial. Materialism also may be used to describe a way of life based on fulfilling material pleasures and bodily comforts and ignoring the satisfaction of spiritual needs.

The natural sciences deal only with the visible world, follow a sensory and experimental approach, and tend to accept only those conclusions resulting from their approach. Thus, the modern scientific worldview is quite similar to materialism. In other words, individual scientists may believe in God and the existence of immaterial entities like the spirit, whereas the modern scientific approach is by nature materialistic. For that reason, scientific materialism has the potential of being even more dangerous than materialistic philosophy. Philosophical ideas can be set aside as theories having little or no influence on one's daily life. In contrast, people must think, believe, and act in line with scientific conclusions.

Scientific materialism has a considerable effect on how we order our lives. For example, if people do not believe in a Day of Reckoning conducted by a Supreme Being Who knows everything about us and will call us to account, or believe that they are free to design their own laws and lives according to the requirements of a short, transient life, what should we expect? If being *scientific* means to deny or at least doubt the existence of anything metaphysical, and if *scientific* knowledge causes spiritual and metaphysical knowledge to be seen as superstitions, people have no alternative other than to live as materialists.

Given this, scientific materialism and the practical materialism it produces are responsible, along with philosophical materialism and communism, for the global erosion of morals and spiritual values, increasing crime and drug addic-

---

9 ibid, "10th Word" and the "12th Word"; Fethullah Gülen, *The Essentials of the Islamic Faith*, The Light, Inc., New Jersey: 2005; Also see Dr. Suat Yildirim, "Worldwide Corruption by Scientific Materialism," *Islamic Perspectives on Science*, Kaynak, Izmir: 1998.

tion rates, and the unjust exploitation of the weak. They are also behind ongoing ruthless colonialism, now disguised, and other modern social and political crises.

Scientific materialism does not deny, theoretically, the existence of immaterial truths; rather, it says that anything immaterial cannot be known. You can discuss God's existence or any metaphysical topic with such people. But since scientific materialism argues that only material things can be known, it diverts our attention from immaterial truths. One result of this view is agnosticism, the belief that nothing can be known about God or of anything except material things. Scientific materialism, because it tends to explain immaterial truths in material terms and therefore reduces quality to quantity and spiritual to physical, is responsible for the rise of most modern false beliefs and "mystical" practices. This is seen most clearly in psychology, psychiatry, and psychoanalysis.

Practical materialism, to which scientific materialism gave birth, is now the dominant global worldview irrespective on one's religion or lack thereof. When development is mentioned, most people instantly think of economic development and the betterment of worldly life, and so give precedence to worldly life. And since material wealth and resources cause rivalry among peoples and countries, not a day passes without some clash occurring somewhere in the world.

Even if we leave out all human values, lofty truths and ideals, and spiritual happiness sacrificed for material development, the modern civilization engendered by scientific materialism has caused great harm. The products of science are usually exploited by the great powers to consolidate their dominion over the world. In addition, developments in genetics, biology, physics, and chemistry threaten the very existence of humanity.

Modern civilization, as pointed out by Said Nursi is founded upon five negative principles[10]:

• Power, which tends to be used to oppress others.
• Self-interest, the pursuit of which causes people to chase after what they want to possess. This gives rise to rivalry and competition.
• Life as struggle, a view that leads directly to internal and external conflict.

---

10 Said Nursi, *The Letters*, Truestar, London: 1995, Vol. II, p. 310.

- Unity based on racial separatism. This is realized by swallowing up other people's resources and territories. Such racism also leads to terrible collisions between peoples.
- Satisfaction (whether real or not) of novel caprices or aroused desires. This brutalizes people.

Modern materialistic civilization stimulates consumption and so continually engenders and increases new, artificial needs. Its demands can be imposed via propaganda, advertisements, and their support of such undesirable human tendencies as "keeping up with the Jones." The resulting paradigm of "producing to consume and consuming to produce" destroys a person's delicate balance and causes extraordinary increases in mental and spiritual illnesses. Such a life has no place for spiritual profundity or true intellectual activity. In fact, it places intellect in the service of pragmatism and earning more money and other things (e.g., awards, recognition, and rewards).

It is highly questionable whether scientific and economic developments have brought happiness to humanity, whether developments in telecommunications and transportation have provided humanity with what it needs. It is highly questionable whether modern people have found true satisfaction and solve their problems. Do their needs not increase day by day? While people in the past needed a few things to lead a happy life, does not modern life make people feel the need of some new things every day? To satisfy each new need requires more effort and production which, in turn, stimulates more consumption. This leads people to regard life as a course or process of struggle, and gives rise to a cruel rivalry and competition. So it follows that because might is right in such a world, only the powerful have the "right" to survive. Such attitudes lie behind such Western philosophical attitudes or so-called scientific theories as Darwinian evolution and natural selection, historicism, and the like.

We do not belittle or condemn scientific study and accomplishment. On the contrary, we welcome them enthusiastically as signs and confirmation of humanity's superiority to angels. As the Qur'an states, God created humanity to rule on the Earth in conscious, deliberate conformity with God's commands (2:30-31). Although humanity has been honored with free will, it is not compelled to do anything. Thus, to allow individuals to fulfill the reason for their creation, God gave them the knowledge of things and thereby made them superior to angels. However, if scientific study is to be directed toward humanity's real benefit, it must be pursued within the guidance of immaterial, metaphysical, and God-given rules.

MODERN PEOPLE IN THE SWAMP OF MODERN MATERIALISTIC LIFE

The European Renaissance developed in opposition to the then-current world-view of religion and its views of humanity, life, things, and art.

Aldous Huxley's *Brave New World*, published in 1932, has been becoming more of a reality and less a satirical fantasy. In this world, human beings are produced, classified, and conditioned in tubes according to their future social functions as Alpha, Beta, Gamma, Delta, and Epsilon types. The Old World's traditional values and feelings, such as fatherhood, motherhood, kinship, love, sacrifice, altruism, and chastity, have been replaced. Having freed humanity from religion, morality, thought, art, production sufficient for a moderate life, and sharing and mutual helping, this new world reduces the individual and community to the functions of consumption, entertainment, and stability.

As Alexis Carrel says in *Man: This Unknown*,[11] in the modern world established by engineers under the guidance of scientists, people live in cities containing factories, offices, schools, and amusements. Their houses and offices are no longer dark and dingy. Modern heating and lighting keep the temperature at the desired level, and measures have been taken against changes in weather. They are no longer oppressed by freezing storms or suffocating heat, or have to walk to and from work. Distances have diminished and, thanks to developments in transportation and communication, the world now resembles a big village. Wide highways, comfortable houses, air-conditioning, washing machines, refrigerators, electrical and electronic appliances, modern bathrooms, luxurious cars, computers, and telecommunicative devices incite modern people to sing songs of victory over traditional values and nature.

Modern people have still not achieved everything. For instance, they have not solved the mysteries of their ego, discovered what it means to be human, or perceived that humanity is a part of the natural environment to which they are related with unbreakable ties. As Mephisto says in Goethe's *Faust*, when one attempts to know any living being, what he or she does first is to drive away its spirit.

Muhammad Iqbal described the natural sciences as a flock of vultures crowding around nature's flesh and, after each picking a part of it, flying off. In order to meet its ever-increasing needs, humanity has spent a great deal of time and effort to develop the natural sciences. However, it has yet to grasp the fact

---

11 Turkish translation by R. Özdek, Istanbul: 1983.

that its scientists still cannot create a blade of grass, a gnat's wing, or a living cell.

Sometimes, like many Existentialist philosophers, they feel like stones cast down aimlessly on this planet, see the world as devoid of intellect, the heavens as devoid of feeling, existence as meaningless, and regard sacrifice as equal to suicide. They thought they could overcome life's threats and worries by living and cooperating with others, but their selfishness and materialism does not allow them to do this with any sincerity. Rejecting God, they have deified their egos and replaced their God-given freedom with their pursuit of worldly enjoyment and desire, and the manipulations of those who try to continue their dominion at all costs. They also have submitted their honor and dignity to consumption, luxury, and cynicism.

Seeking to discover themselves by rejecting servanthood to God (as Erich Fromm explains) in order to be themselves and attain their true freedom, modern people still cannot escape their innate realities and requirements, or be freed from their need and emotions of worship. Fromm points out that modern people have numerous fetishes, more deities or idols than "primitive" peoples.[12] Causality (nature) means to attain something. Desire, ambition, power-seeking, and lust are modern deities. Fetishism, totemism, ritualism, self-dedication to a party or state, and idolizing certain people are some aspects of their modern "religion."

The Prophets of revealed religions have been replaced by politicians, sports and movie stars, stage and cinema personalities, and those who set fashions. Although modern people believe they are in control (of life and thinking), they are little more than robots programmed by the mass media and the oppressive minority that own them. Banks, cinemas, universities, nightclubs, stadiums, and factories are the temples of modern religion.

There are walls between people today; a human being is a wolf to a human being. Relations between people are no longer human, for they see each other as a tool to use, an enemy to remove, or a rival to defeat. Market laws direct relations between people. In the capitalist's view, a human being is only a machine, a means of production, an object to exploit. Modern people sell themselves like merchandise. Manual workers sell their labor, while businessmen and women, doctors, and officials sell their skills. The answers given to such questions as "What is your occupation?" and "How much do you earn?" deter-

---

12 A. Yörükan (trans.), *Escape from Freedom* (Istanbul: 1982); A. Aritan (trans.), *Psychoanalysis and Religion* (Istanbul: 1981).

mine one's social standing and value. Self-respect is based on someone else's opinion, and not being liked by others means being non-existent.

People used to live together with their families and near relatives. Now, as Fromm states, they seek to overcome their weakness and helplessness by seeking refuge in trade unions, monopolist capital, weapons, or other such things. Multi-national companies continually gnaw away at humanity so they can earn more. People are lost in supermarkets, and in cities are reduced to nothingness among skyscrapers. The sounds coming from television, radio, and cassette players do not allow them to speak. Advertisements directed toward their desires and passions stimulate consumption and determine their tastes and choices.

Contemporary arts, modern sociopolitical systems, such philosophies as existentialism and structuralism, class consciousness, superior-race theories, new-world-order theses and fantasies, or humanity's tendency toward destruction cannot satisfy modern people. We play the role of a Faust who studied not theology but modern science. In such an atmosphere, neither Satanism nor false beliefs and practices (e.g., necromancy, transcendental meditation, reincarnation, sorcery, and fortune telling, so-called mystical movements, or false occult sciences) can replace the true religion. Nor can they give to modern people who, by losing their true human identity, freedom and personality, have fallen to the lowest depths, the possibility of ascending to the heaven of true humanity.

LIFE WITH AND WITHOUT BELIEF, PARTICULARLY BELIEF IN THE HEREAFTER[13]

The following comparison (by Said Nursi) shows the difference between a life with belief and a life without belief, particularly in the Hereafter:

> In an imagined vision, I was standing on an awe-inspiring bridge set over a deep valley between two mountains. The whole world was completely covered by a thick darkness. As I happened to look to my right, I had the vision of a huge tomb. When I looked to my left, I felt as if I were seeing violent storms and calamities being prepared amid the tremendous waves of darkness. Then, I looked down over the edge of the bridge and I imagined I was seeing a very deep precipice.

---

13 Said Nursi, *The Words*, "23rd Word."

In that dreadful darkness, I had recourse to my torch. Through its dim light a very dreadful scene was shown to me. All along the length of the bridge, such horrible dragons, lions and monsters appeared that I wished I had not had that torch. Whichever way I directed it, I got the same fright. "This torch brings me only trouble," I exclaimed, and I angrily cast it to the ground and broke it. Then, all of a sudden, the darkness disappeared and everywhere was illuminated; it was as if I had switched on a huge light by breaking my torch, and I saw everything in its true nature.

I discovered that the bridge was, in reality, a highway on a smooth plain. The huge tomb on the right was a green, beautiful garden in which the assemblies of worship, prayer, glorification and discourse were being held under the leadership of illustrious persons. The scenes on the left which I had previously imagined to be turbulent, stormy, frightening precipices now appeared as a banqueting hall, a shaded promenade, a very beautiful resting place behind lovely mountains. I realized that what I had imagined to be horrible monsters and dragons were, in fact, domesticated animals such as camels, sheep and goats. "Praise and thanks be to God for the light of belief," I said, and then awoke reciting: *God is the Protecting Friend of those who believe. He brings them out of the layers of darkness into the light* (2:257).

Those two mountains that I saw in my imagined vision are, in reality, the beginning and the end of this life and the life between death and the Resurrection. The bridge is the life-span, between the two phases of the past (on the right) and the future (on the left). The torch is humanity's conceited ego that, relying on its own achievements, does not heed the Divine Revelation. What had looked to me first to be monsters are the events of the world and the extraordinary creatures in it.

Thus, those who have fallen into the darkness of misguidance and heedlessness because of their confidence in their own ego resembles me in the former state—in the dim light of a torch. With their inadequate and misguided knowledge, they see the past as a huge tomb in the darkness of extinction; they see the future as a stormy scene of terror controlled by coincidence or chance. The torch shows them events and creatures as harmful monsters. However, in reality they are subjugated to the All-Wise and the All-Merciful and, in submission to His Decree, fulfill specific functions and serve good purposes. Thus they are the ones referred to in: *As to those who disbelieve, their protecting friends are false deities. They bring them out of light into layers of darkness* (2:257).

If, however, such people are favored with Divine guidance, and belief enters their hearts and their Pharaoh-like egos are broken, if they listen to the Book of God, then they will resemble me in my later state. All of a sudden the whole of the universe will be filled with Divine Light, demonstrating the meaning of: *God is the light of the heavens and the Earth* (24:35).

Then they see through the eye of their hearts that the past is not a huge tomb. Rather, each past century is the realm of authority of a Prophet or a saint, where purified souls, having completed the duties of their lives (worship), with the words, "God is the Greatest!" on their tongues, flew to higher abodes on the side of the future. Looking to their left and through the light of belief, they discern a feasting place set up by the All-Compassionate One at the palaces of bliss in the gardens of Paradise behind the mountain-like revolutions of the intermediate world [the world between this one and the next] and the next life. They are convinced that the storms, earthquakes, epidemic diseases, and the like serve specific functions, just as they understand that spring rain and winds, for example, despite their apparent violence, serve many agreeable purposes. In their view, even death is seen as the beginning of eternal life, and the grave as the gateway to eternal happiness.

A REFLECTION (BY SAID NURSI) ON LIFE WITH AND WITHOUT BELIEF IN THE RESURRECTION[14]

O Master! Heedlessly not trusting in You, but in reliance on my own power and will, I looked around in all six directions, searching for a cure for my pains. Alas, I could find no cure for them. However, it occurred to me: "Isn't it enough for you that you have pains as cure?"

In heedlessness I looked to past time on my right to find solace, but yesterday appeared to me in the form of my father's grave and past time as the huge tomb of my forefathers. It filled me with horror rather than consolation. [Belief shows that huge, terrifying tomb to be a familiar and illuminated meeting place for the gathering of friends.]

---

14 ibid, 17th Word.

Then, I looked to the future on the left. I could find no cure. Rather, tomorrow appeared to me in the form of my grave and the future as the large tomb of my contemporaries and the forthcoming generations; it gave me no feeling of familiarity but of fright. [Belief and the peace provided by belief show that frightful large tomb to be a feast of the Most Merciful in delightful palaces of bliss.]

Since no good appeared from the left either, I looked at the present day, and I saw it like a coffin, carrying my desperately struggling corpse. [Belief shows that coffin to be a place of business and a glittering guesthouse.]

As I could find no cure from that direction either, I raised my head and looked at the top of the tree of my life. I saw that its single fruit was my corpse; it was looking down at me from the top. [Belief shows that fruit to be the spirit, which is to be favored with eternal happiness in an eternal life and has left its worn-out home to travel among the stars.]

Despairing of that direction, I lowered my head. I looked and saw that the dust of my bones underfoot had mixed with the dust of my first creation. Giving no cure, it rather increased my pains. [Belief shows that dust to be the door to Mercy and the curtain over the windows of the hall of Paradise.]

Turning away from that direction, I looked behind and saw a temporary world with no foundation revolving in valleys of nothingness and darkness of non-existence. Not relieving my pains, it rather added to them the poison of more gloom and terror. [Belief shows that world revolving in darkness to be missives of the Eternally-Besought-of-All and sheets of Divine inscriptions that, having completed their duties and expressed their meanings, have left their results for a new existence in place of themselves.]

Since I saw no good from that direction either, I cast my eye ahead of me. I saw that the door of my grave stood open at the end of my way, behind which the highway leading to eternity caught my eyes from afar. [Belief shows the door of the grave to be the portal to the world of light, and that way to lead to eternal happiness, and thus provides a salve and a cure for my pains.]

Thus, rather than consolation and a feeling of familiarity, I received only horror and a feeling of desolation from these six directions. Further, apart from an insignificant free will, I have nothing with which to resist or oppose them. [However, belief provides a document for relying on an Infinite Power. It causes the willpower to be employed in the name of God. It also makes it able to withstand anything, just like a soldier who, using his insignificant power on behalf of the state, can perform deeds thousands of times greater than his own power. Since belief gives its reins to the heart and the spirit, and not to the hands of the animal body, it can penetrate the past and the future, for the sphere of life of the heart and spirit is broad.]

BELIEF IN THE RESURRECTION MAKES DEATH LOVABLE

The All-Compassionate Creator has made this world in the form of a festival, a place of celebration and exhibition. He has decorated it with the most wonderful inscriptions of His Names, and clothed each spirit with a body possessing suitable and appropriate senses that allow the individual to benefit from the good things and bounties in the festival. He sends each spirit to this festival for one time. As it is very extensive in regard to time and space, He divided it into centuries and years, seasons and days, and various parts. His animal and plant creations promenade therein, especially during the spring and summer, when the Earth's surface is transformed into a vast arena of successive festivals for all small creatures. This arena is so glittering and attractive that it draws the gaze of angels, other inhabitants of the heavens, and spirit beings in the higher abodes. For people who think and reflect, it is an arena for reflection, and one so wonderful that the mind cannot describe it.

The manifestations of Divine Grace, Mercy, and Liberality in this Divine festival are counterbalanced by the Names of All-Overwhelming, All-Crushing, and One Who Causes to Die through death and separation. This does not appear to be in line with the all-embracing Mercy expressed in *My Mercy encompasses all things* (7:156). However, consider the following points:

- After each group of creatures has served its purpose and produced the desired results, the All-Compassionate Creator causes most of them, by His Compassion, to feel weariness and distaste with the world. He then grants them a desire to rest and a longing to emigrate to another world. And so when they are discharged from their duties (through death), He arouses in them an enthusiastic inclination to return to their original home.

- The Most Merciful One bestows the rank of martyrdom on a soldier who dies in the line of duty (defending sacred values), and rewards a sheep sacrificed in His way with an eternal corporeal existence in the Hereafter. Given this, His infinite Mercy assigns a specific reward and wage, according to their nature and capacity, to other animate beings who perform their duties despite hardship and death. Thus, these beings are not sad when death comes; rather, they are pleased and look forward to it.

The world is continually enlivened through creation and predetermination, and ceaselessly stripped of life through other cycles of creation, determination, and wisdom. Death is not extinction, but a door opening on a better, more developed, and more refined life.

The Qur'an presents death as something created and therefore having existence (67:2). When death enters a living body, life seems to depart. In reality, however, that organism is being elevated to a higher degree. The death of a plant, the simplest level of life, is a work of Divine artistry, just like its life, but one even more perfect and better designed. When a tree seed "dies," it appears to decompose into the soil. However, it actually undergoes a perfect chemical process, passes through predetermined states of re-formation, and grows into an elaborate, new tree. A "dead" seed represents the beginning of a new tree, and shows that death is something created (like life) and, accordingly, is as perfect as life.

Since fruit and animals, when consumed by people, cause them to rise to the degree of human life, their deaths can be regarded as more perfect than their lives. If this is true of plants, it must be true of people. As people are the pinnacle of creation, their deaths must be more perfect and serve a still greater purpose. Once individuals have died and been buried, they surely will be brought into eternal life.

Death is a blessing for human beings for several reasons, among them[15]:

- It discharges us from the hardships of life, which gradually become harder through old age. It also opens the gates to reunion with many of our friends who died before us.
- It releases us from worldly life that is a turbulent, suffocating, narrow dungeon of space, and admits us into the wide circle of the Eternal

---

15 Said Nursi, *The Letters*, "1st Letter."

Beloved One's mercy. As a result, we enjoy a pleasant and everlasting life free from suffering.

- Old age and other unbearable conditions are ended through death. Both the elderly and their families benefit from this. For example, if your elderly parents and grandparents were living in poverty and hardship, would you not consider their deaths to be blessings? The autumnal death of insects is a mercy for them, for otherwise they would have to endure winter's harshness and severity and be deprived of their lovers: lovely flowers.

- Sleep brings repose and relief, as well as mercy, especially for the sick and afflicted. Death, sleep's brother, is a blessing and mercy particularly for those afflicted with misfortunes that might make them suicidal. As for the misguided, death and life are a torment within torment and pain after pain.

- Just as death is a blessing for a believer, the grave is the door to illuminated worlds. This world, despite its glitter, is like a dungeon in comparison with the Hereafter. To be transferred from the dungeon of this world to the gardens of Paradise, to pass from the troublesome turmoil of bodily life to the world of rest and the realm where spirits soar, to be free of the distressing noise of creatures and go to the Presence of the Most Merciful—all of this is a journey, indeed a happiness, to be desired most earnestly.

- The All-Merciful One explains in His Scriptures, especially the Qur'an, the true nature of the world and the life therein, and warns us that love or attachment to either one is pointless.

THE WORLD WITH ITS THREE FACETS[16]

The world and things have three facets. These are the following:
- Its first facet turns to the Divine Names and Attributes. Each created thing is a manifestation of certain Divine Names and Attributes, such as Mercy, Creativity, Grace, Provision, Favoring, Hearing, Seeing, or Speaking. As this facet only mirrors those Names and Attributes, it does not experience decay and death, but is continually refreshed and renewed.

---

16 Ibid., "24th Letter."

- Its second facet turns to the Hereafter—the world of permanence. Being like a field sown with the seeds of the Hereafter, seeds that will grow into permanent "trees" with permanent fruits, this facet serves the World of Permanence by causing transient things to acquire permanence. It also does not experience decay and death, but life and permanence.

- Its third facet relates to our bodily desires. Many people love this facet, which is the marketplace of sensible conscious persons and a trial for the duty-bound. This facet is apparently the object of decay and death. However, in its inner dimension, there are manifestations of life and permanence to heal the sorrows brought by death, decay, and separation.

Why is love for this third facet not something to be approved? Consider the following:

- The world is a book of the Eternally-Besought-of-All. Its letters and words point not to themselves, but to their Author's Essence, Names, and Attributes. This being so, learn its meaning and adopt it; abandon its decorations and go.

- The world is a field for the Hereafter, so plant it to harvest in the Hereafter. Pay attention to the crop that you will receive in the Hereafter, and throw away the useless chaff.

- The world is a collection of "mirrors" that continually follow each other to reflect their Creator and then pass on. Therefore, know the One Who is manifested in them. See His lights, understand the manifestations of His Names appearing in them, and love the One they signify. Cease your attachment to "those fragments of glass" that are doomed to break and perish.

- The world is a moving place of trade. Do your business and leave. Do not tire yourself in useless pursuit of caravans that leave you behind and ignore you.

- The world is a temporary place of recreation. Study it to take lessons and warnings, but ignore its apparent, ugly face and pay attention to its hidden, beautiful face looking to the Eternal All-Gracious One. Go for a pleasant and beneficial recreation and then return. When the scenes displaying those fine views and beautiful things disappear, do not cry or be anxious.

• The world is a guesthouse. Eat and drink within the limits established by the Munificent Host Who built it, and offer thanks. Act and behave in accordance with His Law. Then depart from it without looking back. Do not interfere in it, or busy yourself in vain with things that one day will leave you and are no concern of yours.

Through such plain truths, He reveals the world's real character and makes death less painful. He makes death desirable for those awake to the truth, and shows that there is a trace of Mercy in all His actions.

BENEFITS OF BELIEF IN THE AFTERLIFE FOR SOCIETY AND PEOPLE

Belief in the afterlife is the bedrock of social and individual human life, the foundation of all felicity and achievement, because after belief in God, belief in the Resurrection has the primary place in securing a peaceful social order. If we do not believe that we will be called to account for our deeds, why should we be expected to live an honest, upright life? But if we act according to the conviction that we will have to give such an account, we will live a disciplined and upright life. The Qur'an declares:

> In whatever affair you may be, and whichever part of the Qur'an you recite, and whatever deed you do, We are witness over you when you are deeply engrossed therein. Not an atom's weight in the earth and in the heaven escapes your Master, nor is there anything smaller or greater, but it is in a Manifest Book. (10:61)

Whatever we do is recorded by angels entrusted with that task. In addition, God has complete knowledge of all our deeds, intentions, thoughts, and imaginings. An individual who lives in full consciousness of this will find true peace and happiness in both worlds; a family and community made up of such individuals will be as if living in Paradise.

Children are sensitive and delicate, very susceptible to misfortune, and easily affected by what befalls themselves and their families. When a family member dies or they are orphaned, their world darkens and they experience great distress and despair. One of my sisters died during my childhood. I was so upset that I frequently went to her grave and asked God from the bottom of my heart: "O God! Please bring her back to life again and let me see her beautiful face once more, or let me die so as to be reunited with her!" So, what else other than belief in the Resurrection, in reunion with the loved ones who emigrated to the other world, can compensate for the loss of parents, siblings, and friends? Only when a child is convinced that his or her loved one has flown to Paradise, to a much better life than this, and that one day they will be reunited, will he or she find true consolation and begin to heal.

How can you compensate the elderly for their past years, their long-ago childhood and youth? How can you console them for the loss of their loved ones, friends, spouses, children or grandchildren who went to the other world before them? How can you remove from their hearts the fear of death and the grave, which is coming closer every day? How can you make them forget death, which they feel so deeply? Can you console them with ever-new pleasures of life? Only when they understand that the grave, an apparent open-mouth dragon waiting for them, is really a door to another, much better world, or a lovely waiting-room to that world, will they feel compensated and consoled for their losses.

The Qur'an voices the feelings of the old through Prophet Zechariah:

> This is a mention of your Master's mercy unto His servant Zechariah; when he invoked Him with a secret, sincere call, saying: "My Master, my very bones have become rotten and my head is shining with grey hair. My Master! I have never been disappointed in my prayer to You." (19:2-5)

Fearing that his kinsmen would not be sufficiently loyal to his mission after his death, Zechariah asked his Master for an heir to his mission with that heart-rending appeal. This is the cry of all old people. Belief in God and the Resurrection gives the elderly the good news:

> Do not be afraid of death. Death is not eternal extinction, but only a change of worlds, a discharge from the distressing duties of the worldly life, and a passport to an eternal world where all kinds of beauties and blessings are waiting for you. The Merciful One Who sent you to the world, and has kept you alive therein for such a long time, will not leave you in the darkness of the grave and dark corridors opening on the other world. He will take you to His Presence and grant to you an eternal, ever-happy life. He will bless you with bounties of Paradise.

Only such good news can truly console the elderly and cause them to welcome death with a smile.

Humanity is a unique part of creation, for people can use their free will to direct their lives. Free will is the manifestation of Divine Mercy. If our free will is used properly by doing good deeds, we will be rewarded with the fruits of Mercy. Belief in the Resurrection is a most important and compelling factor that urges us to use our free will in the right way and refrain from sin and from wronging and harming others.

When Caliph 'Umar saw a young man bravely protest and resist a wrong, he said: "Any people deprived of their young people are doomed to extinction." Young people have a transforming energy. If you let them waste that energy in trivial things and self-indulgence, you undermine your nation's future. Belief in the Resurrection prevents young people from committing atrocities and wasting their energies on passing pleasures, and directs them to lead a disciplined, useful, and virtuous life.

Belief in the Resurrection is also a source of consolation for the ill. Suffering from an incurable illness, a believing patient thinks: "I am going. No one can make me live longer. Fortunately, I am going to a place where I will enjoy eternal health and youth. Everyone is doomed to go die anyways." Such a belief has caused the beloved servants of God, Prophets and saints, to welcome death with a joyful smile. Prophet Muhammad said as he was dying: "O God! I desire the eternal company in the eternal world."

He had informed his Companions one day before: "God allowed one of His servants to choose between enjoying the beauties of the world as long as he wishes and what is with Him. The servant chose what is with Him." The servant in question was the Messenger himself. The Companions understood and burst into tears.

Similarly, when Caliph 'Umar was ruler of a vast area stretching from the western frontiers of Egypt to the Central Asia steppes, he prostrated to God and sighed: "I can no longer fulfill my responsibility. Make me die and take me to Your Presence." This desire to go to the other world, the world of eternal beauty, and being blessed with the vision of the Eternally Beautiful One caused the Prophet, 'Umar, and many others to prefer death to life in this world.

The world is a mixture of good and evil, right and wrong, beauty and ugliness, oppressor and oppressed. Many wrongs go unnoticed, and numerous wronged people do not recover their rights. Only their belief in the Resurrection into a world of absolute justice consoles such people and prevents them from seeking vengeance. The afflicted and those suffering misfortune also find consolation, for they believe that whatever befalls them erases some of their sins, and that what they have lost will be restored to them in the Hereafter as a blessing, just as if they had given these items as alms.

Belief in the Resurrection changes a house into a garden of Paradise. In a house where the young pursue their pleasures, children ignore religious sentiment and practices, parents are engrossed in procuring ever more possessions, and grandparents are sent to a poorhouse or a nursing home, or left to shower their love on pets instead of grandchildren, life is a heavy burden. Belief in the Resurrection reminds everyone of their responsibilities toward each other, and engenders a fragrance of mutual love, affection, and respect.

Belief in the Resurrection leads to mutual love and a deeper respect on the part of spouses. Love based on physical beauty is temporary, and therefore of little value. It usually disappears shortly after the marriage. But if the spouses love each other and believe that their marriage is eternal, and that in the other world they will be eternally young and beautiful, their love for each other will not disappear as they age and lose their good looks. If family life is based on belief in the Resurrection, family members will feel as if they are living in Paradise. If a country's social order is based on belief in the Resurrection and the Day of Judgment, life in that country will be far better than what Plato imagined in his *Republic* or al-Farabi (Alpharabios) in his *Al-Madinat al-Fadila* (The City of Virtues). It will be like Madina in the time of the Prophet, or the Muslim lands under the rule of Caliph 'Umar.

A WARNING AND LESSON GIVEN TO A GROUP OF UNHAPPY YOUNG PEOPLE[17]

(Said Nursi writes:)

> One day a number of bright young people came to me, seeking an effective deterrent to guard them against the danger arising from modern worldly life, youth, and animalistic desires. As I had previously told other young people who sought help, I also said to them:

> Your youth will definitely disappear. If you do not restrict yourselves within the limits of what is lawful, it will be lost. Rather than pleasure, it will bring you suffering and calamities in this world, in the grave, and in the Hereafter. If, under Islamic discipline, you use the blessings of youth in gratitude, chastely and uprightly, and in worship, it will in effect remain perpetually and be the cause of gaining eternal youth.

---

17 Said Nursi, *The Words*, "13rd Word."

Life without belief, or belief that has become ineffective because of rebelliousness, produces pain, sorrow, and grief far exceeding the superficial, fleeting enjoyment and pleasure it brings. As intelligent, thinking creatures, all human beings are (in contrast to animals) intrinsically connected to the past and the future, as well as to the present time. They derive both pain and pleasure from them. Since animals do not think, neither sorrow arising from the past nor fear and anxiety concerning the future spoil their present pleasure.

But if people fall into misguidance and heedlessness, sorrow arising from the past and anxiety about the future mar their particular pleasures and dilute them with pain. Any illicit pleasure is like poisonous honey. This means that, with respect to the enjoyments of life, human beings are far lower than animals. In fact, for those who are misguided and heedless, their whole life and existence, their whole world, consists of the day in which they find themselves. According to their misguided belief, all of time past and all past worlds have gone to non-existence. Their intellects, which connect them to the past and the future, produce darkness for them. As they have no belief, the future is also non-existent for them. The separation that becomes eternal because of this non-existence continually darkens their lives.

In contrast, if they build their lives upon belief, then through the light of belief, both the past and the future become illuminated and acquire existence. Like the present time, belief causes them to provide exalted spiritual pleasures and lights of existence for the believers' spirit and heart.

So, that is how life is. If you desire life's pleasure and enjoyment, animate your life with belief and adorn it with religious obligations. Maintain it by abstaining from sin. As for the fearsome reality of death, which is demonstrated by instances of death every day, in every place and time, I shall explain it to you with a parable.

Suppose a gallows has been set up in front of our eyes. Beside it is a lottery office that gives tickets for truly high prizes. There are ten of us and, either willingly or unwillingly, each of us shall be invited there. They may call us (since the appointed time is unknown) at any moment: "Come and mount the gallows for execution!" or "A prize ticket worth millions of dollars has come up for you! Come and collect it!" While we are waiting, two people suddenly appear: One holds and offers some apparently very delicious (but in fact poisonous) sweets for us to eat; the other is honest and solemn. Standing behind the first person, this one says:

"I have brought you a talisman, a lesson. If you study it, and if you do not eat the sweets, you will be saved from the gallows. With this talisman, you will receive your ticket for the matchless prize. You see with your own eyes that those who eat the sweets inevitably mount the gallows. You also see that until they mount the gallows, they suffer dreadful stomach pains from the poisoned sweets. Those who receive the ticket for the large prize seem to mount the gallows. But millions of witnesses testify that they are not hanged; rather, they use the steps to enter the prize arena easily. Look from the windows! The highest officials, the high-ranking persons concerned with this business, announce loudly: "Just as you see with your own eyes those mounting the gallows to be hanged, know that those with the talisman receive the ticket for the prize.""

As in the parable, the dissolute, religiously forbidden pleasures of youth (like poisoned sweets), are the cause of losing belief, the ticket to an eternal treasury and a document for everlasting happiness. Those who eat the sweets are subject to death (like the gallows) and the tribulations of the grave (the door to eternal darkness). The appointed hour (death) is unknown. Therefore its executioner, not differentiating between young and old, may come at any time to cut off your head. If you have given up religiously forbidden pleasures and acquired the Qur'anic talisman (belief and performing religious obligations), 124,000 Prophets, upon them be peace, together with innumerable saints, have proclaimed that you will reach the treasury of eternal happiness. They also have shown the signs and evidences of it.

In short: Youth passes. If wasted in indulgence, it results in countless misfortunes and pains both in this world and the next. If you want to understand how such youths end up in hospitals with mental and physical diseases (mainly for abusing their youth), in prisons or hostels (mainly due to youthful excesses), and in bars (mainly because of the distress provoked by their spiritual unease), go and inquire at the hospitals, prisons, and cemeteries.

You will hear from most hospitals the moans and groans of those who have become dissipated and debauched because of their youthful appetites. From the prisons you will hear the regretful sighs of unhappy people suffering for illicit actions mostly resulting from youthful excess.

And from the graves you will come to know that most of its torments, as testified to by saints who can discern what happens therein, and affirmed by exacting scholars of truth, are the result of a misspent youth.

Ask the old and the sick, who form a considerable part of humanity. The great majority of them will answer you with grief and regret: "Alas! We wasted our youth in frivolity, indeed harmfully. Be careful! Never do as we did!" People who waste their lives in illicit pleasures while they are young subject themselves to years of grief and sorrow in this world, torment and harm in the Intermediate Realm, and severe punishment in the Hereafter.

So, those of you who are addicted to the pleasures of worldly life and, troubled about your future, struggle to secure it and your lives! If you want pleasure, delight, happiness, and ease in this world, be content with what is religiously lawful. That is enough for you. You must have understood from your experiences that in each forbidden pleasure lies a thousand pains. If the events of the future—for example, of fifty years hence—were shown in the cinema as they now show past events, those who now are leading dissipated lives would weep with horror and disgust at the things with which they entertain themselves.

A CONSOLATION TO A FATHER ON THE DEATH OF HIS CHILD[18]

My dear brother in religion and fellow traveler on the road to the Hereafter:

The death of your child, my brother, has grieved me, but since the judgment is God's, to accept His decree with resignation is one of the pillars and signposts of belief. May the All-Mighty enable you to endure it in becoming patience, and may He make your deceased child the means of your prosperity in the Hereafter. For my part, I would like to take this opportunity to clarify five points to console God-fearing believers like you, and to give them good tidings.

First point: What the Qur'an means by *immortal children* is this:

---

18 Said Nursi, *The Letters*, "17th Letter."

If a believer's children die before puberty, they will live eternally in Paradise as loveable children. They will forever be the means of happiness and pleasure to their parents, who will enjoy their love for them in their embraces. Some argue that the people of Paradise will enjoy all pleasures except love for children, because Paradise is not the place of generation. However, the Qur'anic expression the *immortal children* indicates that they will be eternally rewarded with the pure affection of their deceased children, whereas in this world that love or affection is restricted to ten years at most and then is wounded frequently by grief and filial ingratitude.

Second point: Once a man was thrown into prison along with his child, for whom he was responsible. Not only did he have to endure his own affliction, but he had to care for his child as well. While he was suffering, the city's compassionate governor sent a messenger with an offer to care for the child in the palace, because the child was his subject. The man's response was the aggrieved cry: "This child is my only means of consolation. I cannot give her up to anybody." His fellow prisoners, however, gave him this advice: "Your grief makes no sense. If you have pity on your child, let her be taken out of this suffocating, dirty prison to a beautiful, spacious palace. If you prefer to have her stay here for your own advantage, consider how much effort it costs you to look after her. It is in your interest to give her to the governor, whose compassion and sympathy she will certainly arouse so that the governor will wish to meet you. The governor will not send her to prison, but instead will summon you to the palace on the condition that you obey and trust in him."

It is as in the parable above, my brother, that all believers whose child or children have died should think thus: (Prepubescent) children are innocent. Their Creator, Who is All-Compassionate and All-Generous, has taken them into His care out of His perfect compassion, whereas I would be unable to give them adequate training in mind or morals. Also, their Creator is much more affectionate toward them that I could be. How happy the children are, since God has taken them out of the wearying life of this world to the highest Heaven. If they had lived longer, they might have been led astray. So I should not grieve. They might have done me some good if they had grown up to be righteous people, but now they are enjoying eternal happiness. In addition, they will be the means of everlasting pleasure for me through parental love, and they will intercede with God for my eternal happiness in Paradise. For this reason, one who obtained a reward a thousand times greater than a reward merely probable should not weep and wail.

Third point: A child is the creature and slave of God, and belongs to Him. God has placed children in their parent's care for a fixed term and for the children's sake. In return, God has put in their hearts pleasure-giving affection toward the children. Therefore believers should not wail for their children when God, the All-Compassionate Creator, takes them away out of His Compassion.

Fourth point: Parents might have some right to wail for a deceased child if the world were eternal and humanity lived forever. But the reality is otherwise, as the world is only a guesthouse. We will all go where these deceased children have gone, for death is not restricted to them alone. As the separation is temporary, and the reunion has already been decided in the intermediate world (between death and the Last Judgement) and Paradise, believers should thank God for everything and endure every calamity in the full conviction that the Judgment is His.

Fifth point: Affection, one of the sweetest and most beautiful manifestations of Divine Compassion, is a kind of water of life that leads humanity to God more quickly than love. As love for temporal beings can change into love for God, although after much difficulty, affection can make one's heart sincerely devoted to God, but without as much difficulty. Parents love their children as much as they love everything connected with their world. If they are believers, they will renounce the world when their children are taken away from them, and completely turn to God. They come to feel great interest in the place where their children have gone and, convinced that the transitory world deserves no heart-felt interest, attain a high spiritual state. Misguided people, however, are in a very poor state after losing their children. They lead dissolute lives in neglect of God's commands, and so are quite dismayed and aggrieved when their children die, for they believe that their children have exchanged a soft bed for the dark soil of the grave. Their disbelief in Paradise, which God has prepared for His servants out of His Compassion, increases their grief. But believers are convinced that the Compassionate Creator of the children has taken them to Paradise out of this foul world, and so endure the children's death with "becoming patience." So do not worry, my brother. This is a temporary separation. Say: The Judgment is God's. We belong to God, and it is to Him that we are returning—and be patient.

CHAPTER 3
RATIONAL AND SCIENTIFIC ARGUMENTS

RATIONAL AND SCIENTIFIC ARGUMENTS[19]

Almost all religions agree that a day will come when the world will be destroyed and rebuilt, and that the dead will be raised to another, eternal life. This belief has been communicated by more than 100,000 Prophets, millions of saints, the great majority of people, and most philosophers and scientists throughout history. However, under the influence of Europe's scientific materialism, which rose in the eighteenth century and permeated almost all the scientific circles in the nineteenth, many people now either doubt or reject this belief. Before proceeding, we will say a few words about denial or rejection.

According to logic, a thing's existence is established when one instance of it is found, whereas its denial or rejection requires a search throughout time and space. Or, two individuals' testimony that the item exists proves that it does exist, while denying it means that it is unknown to all people regardless of time or place. For example, a black swan only has to be seen somewhere once to prove its existence; its denial requires that no one anywhere or at any time has ever seen or ever will see such a creature.

Another example is sighting the new moon. During the Muslim fasting month of Ramadan, one reliable person's sighting of the new moon is accepted over the denial of many others. Why? Establishing the truth of this claimed sighting is based on one "positive" instance of witnessing, whereas denial can be the result of various factors: weak eyesight, a bad location, personal carelessness, and so on.

Consider the following more concrete, historical example. As evidence of his Prophethood, Prophet Muhammad split the moon by a gesture of his index finger. This is a historical event that occurred in front of many Qurayshi unbelievers at midnight. However, there always have been those who deny this event on the grounds that: "If the splitting of the moon had taken place, it would have been known to the whole world and related in all subsequent books of human history." The reality is as follows:

---

19 Except for the scientific arguments, see Said Nursi, *The Words*, "10th Word," and Fethullah Gülen, *The Essentials of the Islamic Faith*, Chapter 4.

Splitting the moon is a miracle. A Prophet works miracles in the presence of those who challenge his Prophethood, and therefore a miracle concerns only those challengers. This is why the moon was split before a certain gathering who did not accept his Prophethood. It happened momentarily at a time of night when people were asleep. Obstacles prevented others from seeing it: mist, clouds, and time differences, among others. Besides, at that time science and civilization were not yet well advanced or widespread, and so not many people watched the skies. Finally, there was nothing to necessitate its visibility all over the world. Thus this miracle was not seen globally or related in other nations' history books.

The example demonstrates that while one or two pieces of evidence are enough to prove or establish something, denial arises from many factors and demands global investigation. This is why denial has no weight in the face of concrete evidence, and why concrete evidence is preferable to the denial of numerous persons.

Moreover, rejection or denial is a conclusion or a judgment. Any conclusion or judgment not arising from evidence has no weight and is not worth considering. Denial of the Resurrection and the afterlife cannot be—and is not—based on any evidence. It is a sheer negation, even a delusion, arising from no rational, logical, or scientific evidence.

Moreover, two specialists are preferable to thousands of non-specialists. Although belief in the Resurrection and the afterlife is based on many rational and scientific arguments, it is a religious matter. The source of religion is, after all, Divine Revelation. As the Prophets receive this Revelation, they are the specialists. More than 100,000 Prophets have come, and all have preached the same pillars of belief, including belief in the Resurrection and the afterlife. Even in today's world, where scientific materialism is widespread and dominates scientific circles, the number of people following a religion and therefore believing in the afterlife is greater than those who deny it.

Some may regard religious beliefs as subjective. If we were to discuss what is really scientific and whether religious beliefs based on Revelation are "subjective" when compared to scientific knowledge, we would be embarking on a long conversation indeed! Unfortunately, such a conversation is beyond the scope of this book. What we point out here is that denial of or skepticism about the afterlife is not objective, for no skeptic (or atheist or agnostic) can use science to objectively prove that skepticism is scientific or that there is no afterlife.

Skepticism, atheism, and agnosticism are personal, subjective beliefs that are subject to fundamental error and complete invalidation. Since a skeptical belief does not have the substance of science, all skeptical or atheistic beliefs are invalid.

RATIONAL ARGUMENTS

Consider the following analogy: Traveling upon a road, you come upon a caravanserai built by a great person. It is decorated with the greatest expense in order to delight and instruct the guests during their night's stay. They can see just a little, for they are staying for a very short time. Briefly tasting the joys of what is offered, they continue their journey unsatisfied. However, the great one's servants busily record each guest's conduct and preserve the record. You see, too, that most of the wonderful decorations are replaced daily with fresh ones for newly arriving guests.

Having seen all this, can any doubt remain that the caravanserai's builder must have permanent exalted dwellings, inexhaustible precious treasures, an uninterrupted flow of unlimited generosity? With his generosity shown here, he intends only to arouse his guests' appetite for what remains in his immediate presence, to awaken their desire for the gifts he has prepared for them.

If you reflect upon this world, you will understand the following:

- This world, just as the caravanserai, does not exist for itself. Neither could it have assumed this shape by itself. Rather, it is a well-constructed temporary place, wisely designed to receive those beings who constantly arrive, stay for a while, and then depart.
- Those dwelling therein are guests, invited by their Generous Sustainer to the Abode of Peace.
- This world's adornments are not here for your enjoyment or admiration, for such temporary pleasures result in long-lasting pain when they disappear. They give you a taste to rouse your appetite. But they do not satiate you, for they are too short-lived, or your life is too short. Such valuable and temporary adornments must be there to instruct you in wisdom, arouse gratitude, and encourage you to seek their permanent originals. In short, the adornments you see are for exalted goals beyond themselves.
- This world's adornments are like samples and forms of blessings stored in Paradise, by the Mercy of the All-Merciful, for people of faith and good conduct.

• These transient objects were not created for non-existence, to appear briefly and then disappear. They were created to be assembled briefly in existence and to acquire the requisite forms so that they could be registered, their images preserved, their meanings understood, and their consequences recorded. We know this because one of the purposes in the realm of permanence is to engender from them everlasting spectacles for the people of eternity. Things have been created for eternity, not for annihilation. Annihilation, which is only apparent, marks a completion of duty and a release from service. But while every transient thing progresses to annihilation in one aspect, in numerous other aspects it remains eternally.

Look at a flower, a word of God's Power. For a short time it smiles upon us, then hides behind the veil of annihilation. It departs in the way a word that leaves your mouth disappears. The word disappears but leaves its meaning in the minds of those who heard it. Likewise, a flower goes but leaves its visible form in the memory of those who saw it and its inner essence in its seeds. It is as if each memory and seed records the flower's adornment, or somehow perpetuates it.

If this is true for a being near the simplest level of life, it will readily be appreciated how closely humanity, the highest form of life and owner of an imperishable soul, is attached to eternity. Again, the laws according to which flowering and fruit-bearing plants are formed, and representations of their forms are most orderly preserved and perpetuated in their seeds despite all external changes, show us how closely the human spirit is attached and related to eternity.[20] Our spirit has a most exalted and comprehensive nature and, though housed in a body, is like a conscious and luminous law issuing from the Divine Command.

• People have not been left to wander at will. The forms and consequences of their deeds, recorded and registered, are preserved for the Day of Judgment.

• The autumnal death of all beautiful creatures seen during the summer and spring does not carry them to nothingness. Rather, it is a discharge from service, an emptying that makes way for the new creatures who will come next spring and assume their functions. Finally, it is a form of Divine warning to rouse conscious beings from their forgetfulness,

---

20 Laws may be likened to spirits, in that they have the same meaning for the life and existence of plants as his or her spirit has for a human being.

to shake them out of the torpor that causes them to neglect their obligation to give thanks.

Nothing in existence is in vain; no act in creation is futile. Consider photosynthesis. A tree's leaves are lungs that separate carbon dioxide into carbon and oxygen during the day. So, they give off oxygen and retain carbon, which then combines with the hydrogen of the water brought up through its roots. Out of such elements, God makes sugar, cellulose and other unique chemicals, fruits, and blossoms. The same carbon dioxide and water contribute to the growth of innumerable kinds of fruit, each of which has a unique taste. This process appears so simple, but even if all people joined together to produce a single fruit, they would fail.

Respiration involves a great deal of energy. However, this very process provides a tree with much more energy than it needs: During the night a tree takes in oxygen and sends out carbon dioxide.

Consider what deliberate results are produced by this unconscious tree's actions. Is it really conceivable that something completely ignorant and unconscious of its own existence, which has no power of choice, can do such comprehensive things that require an all-comprehensive knowledge, power, and choice? The Power that attaches such significant purposes to a tree and makes it the means of many deliberate results will not abandon humanity (the fruit of the tree of creation) to its own devices or condemn it to eternal annihilation.

God created humanity for many deliberate purposes and, without allowing them to remain eternally underground, will resurrect all people in an eternal world. Just as He preserves a fruit in memories and through its seeds, and just as He returns it the next summer after He has promoted it to a higher level of life in an animal or human body, so will He promote humanity to a higher level of life in another world following this one's total destruction.

A human being undergoes an ordered and systematic process of development: from a sperm and an egg to a blood-clot, which then acquires tissues, bones, and flesh. This lump of flesh develops into a unique human being through several very specific stages, each of which has precise principles that indicate the exercise of purpose, will, and wisdom. Each human body, moreover, is renewed each year and sometimes even within 6 months, through a process that replaces decomposed cells with new ones.

These new cells are produced by the body's use of the nutrition we consume to meet each cell's needs. The process is as follows: All elements that made up the food come together from the atmosphere, soil, or water. It seems that they are ordered to go to a specific place, for their movements are so precise and their manner of going so remarkable that a purposeful, predetermined operation is indicated. They start from the inanimate world of elements and chemical substances, and pass to the animated world of vegetables and animals. Having developed into sustenance in agreement with definite principles, they enter the body as food, where they are "cooked" in different "kitchens." When they have been sufficiently transformed and passed through "filters" (e.g., digestive, respiratory, and other filtering organs), they are distributed according to the cells' needs.

These processes follow certain unchanging laws; there is no room for chance, coincidence, nature, and unconscious causes. They all display perfect knowledge, wisdom, and insight. Whenever the needed nourishment enters a cell from its surrounding element, it acts, as if voluntarily, according to the laws specified for that stage and in an orderly manner. It reaches its goal in such an orderly manner that it appears to proceed at the command of an All-Wise Mover. In this way, it advances from stage to stage and level to level. When it reaches its appropriate position, at the command of its Sustainer and without deviating from its aim and object, it establishes itself therein and begins to work.

This entire process manifests an absolute will and determination based on an all-encompassing knowledge. The observed order and arrangement are so perfect that it is as if directions were written on each particle's "forehead." This purposeful wisdom, will, and determination open our eyes to the fact that everything in existence has been created for certain purposes, that we have been sent here for certain tasks, and that most of the fruits of our actions will be displayed in another life.

A plant dies in an animal's stomach and rises to the degree of animal life; an animal is consumed by a person and rises to the degree of human life; a human being drops into earth (after death) to attain a higher degree of life prepared by his or her acts in this life.

God created the world from nothing. Each human being is unique, for they have no pre-existing parts in this world. He builds each individual's body from soil, air, and water, and then transforms them into conscious, intelligent beings. Is it not logical to state that the maker of a machine can destroy it and then reassemble it perfectly, or that a commander can assemble dispersed troops with a trumpet call?

Our resurrection is as easy as this. God Almighty will gather each individual's atoms, regardless of where they are, and grant them a higher, eternal form of life: *Say: "Travel in the land and see how He originated creation, then God brings forth the later growth. Assuredly, God is able to do all things"* (29:20); *Say: "He Who has originated them the first time will bring them to life again (in the Hereafter)"* (36:79); and *it is He Who originates the creation, then brings it back again, and it is easier for Him* (30:27).

Just as rested soldiers regroup themselves more rapidly when the bugle sounds, an individual's essential bodily particles, which had established close relations and familiarity with each other during their worldly existence, reassemble quicker than they did when first created when the Archangel Israfil blows his trumpet. Not all component parts need to be present. Rather, only the fundamental parts and essential particles, which are like nuclei and seeds and called "the root of the tail" (in a Prophetic saying), may be sufficient for the second creation.[21] The All-Wise Creator will rebuild the human body upon this foundation.

Everything is subject to the law of development up to a final end. Given this, everything must evolve to a final end. This means that everything has a limited lifespan and that it will die upon reaching its final end. Since a human being (a microcosm, a conscious miniature of the universe) eventually will die, the universe (a macro-human being) also must perish and be resurrected on the Last Day. Just as a living tree, an unconscious miniature of the universe, cannot save itself from annihilation, so "the branches of creatures" that have grown from "the tree of creation" will die.

If the universe is not destroyed by an external event coming from the Eternal Will, then a day, also predicted by science, will come when it will begin to die. It will give a sharp cry, and the following events will occur: *When the sun shall be darkened; when the stars shall be thrown down; when the mountains shall be set moving* (81:1-3), and *When heaven is split open; when the stars are scattered; when the seas swarm over* (82:1-3).

Consider the following significant, subtle point. Water freezes and loses its essential liquid form, and ice changes into water and loses its essential solid state. An item's essence becomes stronger at the expense of its material form. The spirit weakens as the flesh becomes more substantial, and the flesh weakens as the spirit becomes more illuminated. Thus life gradually refines the

---

21 This bone at the end of our spinal column cannot be consumed by the soil. It may contain our DNA.

solid to the advantage of the afterlife. The Creative Power breathes life into dense, solid, and inanimate substances, and refines that solid world to the advantage of the coming world through the light of life.

A truth never perishes, no matter how weak it is. Instead, it takes form in the corporeal world. As this truth flourishes and expands, its form grows weaker and it becomes more refined. Spiritual truth, which actually constitutes something's essence, is inversely proportional to its form's strength. Therefore, as the form grows denser the truth becomes weaker; as the form grows weaker the truth becomes stronger. This law is common to all creatures destined to develop and evolve. We can conclude from this argument that the corporeal world, which is no more than a form containing the great truth of the universe, will be broken into pieces by the Majestic Creator and then rebuilt in an even more beautiful form. One day, the meaning of *Upon the day the Earth shall be changed to other than the Earth* (14:48) will be realized.

Besides innumerable instances of death and revival or replacement constantly witnessed in nature and in our own bodies, an overall death and revival is repeated every year. During winter, a white "shroud" covers much of the Earth, whose yearly life cycle ends during the autumn. Nature already has turned pale and shows fewer traces of life. The shell has fallen in and, ultimately, trees seem to be no more than hard bones. Grass rots away, flowers wither, migrating birds leave, and insects and reptiles disappear.

But winter is not eternal, for it is followed by a general revival. When the weather becomes warm, trees begin to bud and, wearing their finery, present themselves to the Eternal Witness. The soil swells, and grass and flowers start to blossom everywhere. Seeds that fell into the ground last autumn have germinated and, having annihilated themselves, begin to grow into new forms of life. Migrating birds come back, as do countless insects and reptiles. In short, nature appears before us with all its splendor and finery.

This planet's inhabitants are replaced with other ones every day, every year, and in every age. Those welcomed into this guesthouse leave it some time later and are followed by newcomers. Such deaths and revivals, as well as the subsequent changes and transformations, indicate that the world will die and be replaced with a new one.

The Divine Power can destroy this world with great ease. Consider the following: The universe's constituent parts are connected to each other in countless minute and precise ways in such sublime systems that if a single heavenly body were told to leave its axis, total chaos would result and the universe would begin to die. Stars would collide, planets would be scattered, and the sound of exploding spheres would fill space. Mountains would move, and the Earth would be flattened. This is how the Eternal Power will bring about the next life. By upsetting the universe, the inhabitants of Paradise and Hell will be separated from each other.

A close examination of what goes on in the universe will show that it contains two opposed elements that have spread everywhere, become rooted, and clash with each other. This has resulted in the opposed elements of good and evil, benefit and harm, perfection and defect, light and darkness, guidance and misguidance, belief and unbelief, obedience and rebellion, and fear and love. God kneaded these opposites together like dough, and made the universe subject to the law of alteration and the principle of perfection. The universe manifests, through such a continuous conflict of opposites, incessant alterations and transformations in order to produce the elements of a new world.

One day, the Pen of Divine Destiny will have written what it has to write. The Divine Power will have completed its work, all creatures will have fulfilled their duties and services, and the seeds will have been sown in the field of the afterlife. The Earth will have displayed the miracles of Divine Power, and this transitory world will have hung all the eternal scenes upon the picture-rail of time. The Majestic Maker's eternal Wisdom and Favor will require that the truths of the Divine Beautiful Names' manifestations and the Pen of Divine Destiny's missives be unveiled.

It will be time for all creatures' actions to be repaid, for the truths of the meanings expressed by the Book of the Universe's words to be seen, and for the fruits of potentialities to be yielded. A Supreme Court will be established, and the veil of natural causes will be removed so that everything is submitted directly to the Divine Will and Power. On that day, the Majestic Creator will destroy the universe in order to eternalize it. He will separate the opposites, causing Hell to appear with all its awfulness, and Paradise to appear with all its beauty and splendor.

The Eternal World will be made up of the essential elements of this transitory world, and these elements will be given permanence. Paradise and Hell are the two opposite fruits growing on the tree of creation's two branches, or the chain of creation's two results. They are the two cisterns being filled by the two streams of things and events, the two poles to which beings are flowing in waves. They are the places where Divine Grace and Divine Wrath manifest themselves, and they will be filled up with their inhabitants when the Divine Power shakes the universe with a violent motion.

This point is quite significant. God, the Eternal All-Wise, as required by His Eternal Grace and Wisdom, created this world to test people and to serve as a mirror in which His Beautiful Names are reflected, a vast page on which He writes with the Pen of His Destiny and Power. People are tested to develop their potentialities and thereby manifest their abilities. The emergence of these abilities causes the appearance of relative truths, which, in turn, causes the Beautiful Names of the Majestic Maker to manifest their inscriptions and make the universe a missive of the Eternally-Besought-of-All. This testing also separates the diamond-like essences of sublime souls from the coal-like matter of base souls.

Nothing ever completely disappears. We can record and preserve every word and act of any person on tape; why should we think that God cannot do the same in His own way? Advances in sciences and technology continually provide new evidence for His Existence and Unity, and affirm, together with the Divine origin of the Qur'an, the truth of Islam: *We shall show them Our signs in the outer world and within themselves until it will be manifest to them that (the Qur'an) is the truth. Does not your Master suffice, since He is witness over all things?* (41:53).

If one is sincerely searching for the truth and can "see" it as it is, if one is not blinded by prejudice, ignorance, and worldly aims and desires, every new scientific advance manifests the truth of the Qur'an. We see that God enfolds everything in such small things as seeds. A human being is enfolded in a sperm and egg, or 46 chromosomes. If this number were not 46, he or she would be a completely different being. Similarly when people die, their most essential part (comparable to a plant's seed) does not disappear; rather, God uses it to rebuild them during the Resurrection. God preserves everything. A plant dies during the autumn or winter, but survives in innumerable memories and lives on through its seeds that become plants next spring.

Just as God preserves things in their seeds, He also preserves sounds, voices, appearances, and sights so that they can be displayed in another world. Maybe someday we will discover them while we are still in this world. I remember reading of an experiment conducted by a scientist to identify a killer. The suspects were brought one by one under the tree where the crime was committed. The tree had no "reaction" until the guilty person was brought under it.

The criminal somehow displayed something while committing the crime and it was recorded on the tree.

God, Who preserves a human being in a sperm and an egg, a plant in its seeds, and a chicken in an egg, clearly shows that He records everything by the fact that we can record and preserve sounds and images. Thus, He will not leave humanity to its own devices or allow its records to disappear; rather, He will resurrect all people in a different, eternal world.

The universe is like a huge organism, all of whose parts and "cells" are interrelated and interlinked. In this organism, everything is exactly where it must be and carries out its duties without the slightest neglect. Thus, it displays a perfect, astonishing balance and proportion. It accommodates innumerable species of living and non-living things. Among these species, especially living ones tend to multiply and invade the whole of it, each for its own sake. If, for example, the reproduction of flies and fish and such plants as opium poppies were not controlled and counterbalanced, this balance, proportion, and order could not be maintained. If all flies born during a single spring did not disappear into the ground, they would form a thick cover over the entire Earth.

There is nothing purposeless in the universe. Its ecological system is so complex, and its parts are so interrelated, that the lack or removal of one would result in its destruction. To express this reality, God's Messenger declared: "If dogs were not a community like you, I would order their killing." If the bacteria within trees were killed, we could not obtain fruits from trees. In short, the universe's magnificent, astonishing balance, order, and proportion have been maintained without the slightest disorder for billions of years.

This universal balance and order is the result of universal justice, for every thing is exactly where it must be and does not transgress its limits. However, this same justice cannot be observed in the human realm. Humanity is honored with free will and therefore has to establish justice in social life, but many injustices nevertheless are committed. We observe that hardly any justice is realized: cruel, sinful, and tyrannical persons usually lead comfortable and luxurious lives and depart this world unpunished, while godly, oppressed people endure poverty and difficulty and depart unrewarded. Death makes them equal, with the result that both sides would have departed forever with their deeds unquestioned if there were no supreme tribunal. Being the most basic essential of life and a constant demand of the human conscience, justice requires a tribunal where evil is punished and good is rewarded.

Punishment is sometimes enacted in this world. The disasters endured by past disobedient and rebellious peoples make it clear that people must answer for what they do. But as very little real justice is implemented here, another solution has to be found. Humanity is always subject to whatever correction God Almighty's Splendor and Majesty may choose to apply. So, as declared in: *Keep apart on this day, O you sinners* (36:59), God will separate the good from the wicked in the Hereafter and treat each group according to how they lived in this world. This is simply what justice requires.

The universe works according to a moving timeline. Just as seconds point to minutes, minutes to hours, and hours to today's end and tomorrow's coming, and days point to weeks, weeks to months, months to years, and years to the end of a whole lifespan. Every sphere and dimension of existence has its own days. The appointed lifespan of the universe will one day come to an end.

Also, time is cyclical. For example, a scientist has established that corn is produced abundantly every 7 years, and that fish are abundant every 14 years. The Qur'an points to this fact in *Sura Yusuf*. The life of existence has certain terms or cycles: our worldly life, the life of the grave, and the afterlife, which is the last cycle and has many cycles or terms of its own. The Qur'an calls each of these a day, for a day corresponds to our entire life: dawn, morning, noon, afternoon, and evening correspond to one's birth and infancy, childhood, youth, old age and death, respectively. Night resembles the intermediate life of the grave, and the next morning resembles the Resurrection.

The Earth has a special importance as the universe's heart, center, choice, core, its ultimate end, and very reason for its creation. This is because of the multiplicity of its inhabitants, and because it is the abode, origin, workshop, place of display, and resurrection for uncountable different and constantly changing forms. Despite its small size, it is frequently described as equivalent to the vast heavens: "the Master of the Heavens and the Earth."

Great care is shown in, and many purposes are attached to, even the most insignificant-seeming things. For example, cellulose is a structural tissue that forms the chief part of all plants and trees. Through its elasticity, it enables plants to bend and protects them from breaking. It also has an important place in the paper industry. However, only cud-chewing animals can digest it, for their enzymes secrete a substance that dissolves it. Cellulose also eases excretion by accelerating the bowels and preventing constipation. Cud-chewing animals are like factories that change substances with cellulose into useful matter. Their excrement is used as fertilizer. Innumerable bacteria in the soil consume the excrement, thereby increasing soil productivity and cleansing the soil of bad-smelling things.

In the absence of such bacteria, nothing could survive. Through the manifestation of His Name the All-Purifying, God Almighty employs bacteria to clean the Earth. Have you ever considered why forests are so clean, although many animals die in them every day? It is because carnivorous animals and bacteria consume dead animals and thereby clean the Earth. Could God, Who employs the most insignificant-seeming creatures to serve many great purposes, allow humanity to rot away in the ground, thus reducing its existence to utter futility?

Philosophers, especially Muslim ones, call the universe "a macro-human" and humanity "a normo-" or "micro-cosmos." Like an individual, the universe is an entity consisting of innumerable interrelated parts. Maybe an angel has been deputed to represent the universe, one serving as its spirit. Like humanity, the universe also suffers injuries and, as Einstein puts it, new bodies are formed in its remote corners. Just as each individual has an appointed time of death, so does the universe.

SCIENTIFIC ARGUMENTS

Sciences "walk" on the feet of theories and develop through trial-and-error investigation of those theories. Many current scientific facts once were considered false, just as many previous scientific facts now are known to be fallacies. Also, we accept the existence of many things although we cannot establish their existence scientifically.

Throughout history, most people have believed in an afterlife. So, it would seem to be more scientific to allow for its existence in theory and investigate it. Denying it is unscientific, for such a denial is a conclusion that must be based on concrete proof. No one can prove and therefore scientifically claim the afterlife's non-existence, or that the Resurrection will not take place.

However, developments in experimental science have proven the possibility of restoring humanity to life. A very interesting area of exploration has been opened in this respect, for the issue can be examined with precision for the very first time. This advance is a significant contribution to an improved understanding of this subject. Moreover, it appears that scientific investigations are advancing toward still more highly developed theories. The broader the scope of science becomes, the fewer ambiguities and obscurities there will be.

Materialist scientists once regarded a return to life as impossible, and treated the Resurrection as unworthy of scientific discussion. The first change was brought about by Antoine-Laurent Lavoisier (d. 1794), the celebrated French scientist and founder of modern chemistry. He refuted previous theories by proving to the satisfaction of himself and of his scientific contemporaries that the total quantity and mass of matter in the world neither decreases nor increases.

The discovery of radioactivity and matter's transformation into energy, the second important advance in this area, caused Lavoisier's law to be modified. However, it remains valid as far as the permanence of matter and energy is concerned. Despite the chemical actions and reactions that cause matter to change its form and shape, no element of matter is ever lost. What we see and perceive is a collection of various beings possessing mutable qualities. Such new understandings caused the theory of matter's indestructibility to replace the previous law and to explain fully all of matter's changes and transformations.

Water that falls on the ground and is absorbed, cigarette smoke that rises in the air, fuels consumed by industrial machinery, flames arising from burning wood, a candle that burns and scatters its particles in the air—none of this is utterly lost and destroyed. If we could reassemble their component parts, we would obtain the same original materials without the slightest decrease. It is our superficial way of viewing things, our limited and inadequate way of thinking, that causes us to believe that anything really disappears.

The human body is formed of clay and, after passing beneath the wheels of change and transformation, returns to its original substance. This happens because the body carries an internal receptivity to change. However, its existential core never tends toward non-being as a result of these changes; rather, it loses only the particular nature of its composition, like all other bodies, without sacrificing anything of its essence. Similarly, a human corpse is transformed into clay through the working of internal and external factors. It turns this way and that, each time assuming a new form.

For example, over time a plant may grow over a grave and be eaten by an animal, contributing to its growth. Thus variety is introduced into the matter making up the human body. But the body's substance and content remain firm and indestructible throughout all such changes. Like the different forms taken on by our energy, good and bad deeds are likewise imbued with stability and permanence. They are preserved in the universe's archives, and are the determining factors in our ultimate fate after death.

The efforts of researchers to capture sound waves emitted by previous people have enjoyed some success. To a limited degree and with the help of special equipment, they have recaptured sound waves emitted by toolmakers and imprinted on the tool's surface via their hands' radiation. These scientific accomplishments indicate the reality of the Resurrection. Moreover, they provide a method that, when joined with reflection, may permit us to understand the Resurrection and prove it scientifically.

In addition to these developments, research into such psychic phenomena as out-of-body experiences (OBE), near death experiences (NDE) and death-bed visions (known since ancient times), as well as in instrumental transcommunication (ITC) and electronic voice phenomena (EVP), decisively indicate an afterlife.

Before explaining these phenomena and the latest developments, we will mention the most famous scientists concerned with them and who believed in an afterlife. Among them are such well-known figures as the following:

- Emmanuel Swedenborg (d. 1772): A pioneering scientist in the field of psychic phenomena. A leading scientist of his day, this Swedish scientist wrote 150 works in seventeen sciences. At the University of Uppsala he studied Greek, Latin, several European and Oriental languages, geology, metallurgy, astronomy, mathematics, and economics. He was an intensely practical man who invented the glider, the submarine, and an ear trumpet for the deaf. His view of the universe is remarkably similar to twentieth-century quantum physics: The universe consists of a series of particles in ascending order of size, each of which is composed of a closed vortex of energy spiraling at infinite speeds to give the appearance of solidity.

- Sir William Crookes (d. 1919): A Fellow (later President) of the Royal Society and a co-founder of the Society for Psychic Research (SPR). He discovered six chemical elements, including thallium, and was considered the greatest scientist of his time. After extensive research, he became convinced of the reality of an afterlife. Also in his group were such scientists Master Balfour, Sir William Barrett, Sir Oliver Lodge, and Master Raleigh J. Thompson (discoverer of the electron).

- Thomas Alva Edison (d. 1931): The American inventor of the phono-graph and the electric light bulb, was a spiritualist who experimented with mechanical means of contacting the dead.[22]
- Dr. Glen Hamilton: A twentieth-century investigator, a physician, and member of the Canadian Parliament. In his laboratory, and under strictly controlled conditions, he had a battery of fourteen electroni-cally controlled flash cameras photograph apparitions simultaneously from all angles. Observers included four other medical doctors, two lawyers, one electrical engineer, and one civil engineer. Each witness stated unequivocally that "time after time, I saw dead persons materialize."[23] Baron von Schrenck-Notzing, Professor Charles Richet, Professor Eugene Osty, and Professor Gustav Geley, European scientists active from the early 1900s through the 1920s, also photo-graphed apparitions under controlled laboratory conditions.
- Sigmund Freud (d. 1939): The founder of the psychoanalytic school of psychology. In his dying moments he said that if he had his life to live over, he would study parapsychology.
- Dr. Carl Jung (d. 1961), an internationally known and powerfully influential psychiatrist, admitted that metaphysical phenomena could be better explained by the spirit hypothesis than by any other.[24]
- Another brilliant scientist and inventor who became convinced of the existence of an afterlife was George Meek. When he was 60, he retired as an inventor, designer, and manufacturer of air-conditioning and waste-water treatment devices. His numerous patents allowed him to live comfortably and devote the next 25 years to self-funded, full-time research into life after death.

Meek undertook an extensive library and literature research program, and traveled the world to locate and establish research projects with top medical doctors, psychiatrists, physicists, biochemists, psychics, healers, parapsychologists, hypnotherapists, ministers, priests, and rabbis. He established the Metascience Foundation in Franklin, North Carolina, which sponsored the famous Spiricom research. This research sought two-way instrumental contact between living and dead people.[25]

---

22 *Scientific American*, October 30, 1920.
23 Hamilton, 1977.
24 Jung, *Collected Letters*, Vol. I, p. 431.
25 See the chapter on Instrumental Transcommunication.

Some leaders in life-after-death scientific research are extremely intelligent and astute medical doctors who began their investigation as skeptics. For example:

- Dr Elisabeth Kübler-Ross, who has had a global impact on the treatment of dying people, became convinced of life after death from her close association with thousands of dying patients. As she put it: "Up until then I had absolutely no belief in an afterlife, but the data convinced me that these were not coincidences or hallucinations."[26]

- Dr Melvin Morse, a pediatrician and recognized authority on dying children, was, as he puts it, "an arrogant critical-care physician" with "an emotional bias against anything spiritual." But then his scientific studies of dying children and his extensive study of the literature led him to "the inescapable conclusion" that there is a divine "something" serving as a glue for the universe. He writes:

When I review the medical literature, I think it points directly to evidence that some aspect of human consciousness survives death. Other researchers agree with me. Physician Michael Schroter-Kunhardt, for instance, conducted a comprehensive review of the scientific literature and concluded that the paranormal capacities of the dying person suggest the existence of a time-and-space-transcending immortal soul. Other researchers have reached the same conclusion. Be it through case studies of their own or research they have reviewed, there is in the scientific community a growing belief in the human spirit.[27]

In England a group of scientists, mathematicians, and university professors are publicizing results of experiments on subatomic particles and mathematical calculations that provide a scientific explanation for psychic phenomena.

The late Professor Abdus-Salam, a Nobel Laureate and director of the International Centre for Theoretical Physics, gave financial backing and grants to this group. Central to its claims is the work of Ron Pearson, a former university lecturer in thermodynamics and fluid mechanics. His brilliant *Intelligence behind the Universe* (1990) mathematically confirms the experiments of Crookes, Hamilton, and others. Sam Nichols, an astrophysicist from Leeds University, supports Pearson's calculations and claims that "deceased" entities,

26 Kübler-Ross, 1997, p. 188.
27 Morse, 1984, p. 190.

although composed of slightly different atomic components, exist in and share the same space with the material world.

This is possible because most of what we consider solid matter is, in fact, empty space. Modern physics now teaches that atoms are 99.99999% empty space—the distance between an electron and its nucleus being as great, proportionally, as the distance between the Earth and the sun. Even an atom's electrons, protons, and neutrons now are thought to be energy rather than matter. Astrophysicist Michael Scott of Edinburgh University argues that: "The advancement of quantum physics has produced a description of reality which allows the existence of parallel universes. Composed of real substances, they would not interact with matter from our own universe."

Professor Fred Alan Wolf seems to concur with these findings in his *Mind and the New Physics*, in which he states:

> As fantastic as it sounds, the new physics called quantum mechanics posits that there exists, side by side with this world, another world, a parallel universe, a duplicate copy that is somehow slightly different yet the same. And not just two parallel worlds, but three, four or even more....! In each of these universes, you, I and all the others who live, have lived, will live, and will ever have lived, are alive!

When gathered together, the evidence presented by these and many other scientists shows that there is an afterlife. We have yet to hear of a scientist who can disprove its existence.

Psychic phenomena. Laboratory experiments into psychic phenomena have been conducted for over 100 years, and continue to add more data and objective evidence for the existence of an afterlife. Most impressive and persuasive results have been achieved in controlled experiments where maximum cooperation was achieved between intelligences from this dimension and the afterlife.

One of the first of many eminent scientists to undertake such investigations was Sir William Crookes.[28] Sir William was a skeptic before he was specifically chosen by English skeptics to investigate and discredit psychic phenomena.[29] During his studies, however, he concluded that he had discov-

---

28 Sir William Crookes (d. 1919) was one of the greatest scientists who ever lived. He was showered with honors by England, the United States, Scotland, Germany, France, Italy, South Africa, Holland, Mexico, and Sweden. His contribution to science is unparalleled by any single individual in his and in our modern times.
29 Crookes, 1871.

ered a "new force," to which he gave the name *psychic*. He noted that this force or power was very variable and, at times, entirely absent; it required painstaking and patient investigation. He avoided speculating on the nature of this new force, and appealed to his fellow scientists to help him investigate it.[30]

Hereward Carrington is a most distinguished, highly credible, and respected author who was Director of the American Psychical Institute. He personally investigated many cases of psychic phenomena. In his most impressive work, *The World of Psychic Research* (1973), he outlines several psychic laboratory experiments that prove how intelligences from the afterlife can make their presence and participation known.

For more than 50 years, experimenters have tried to contact deceased people through electronic devices and record their supposed messages. Such contact is proving to be possible and repeatable, is occurring in laboratories throughout the world, and is being subjected to scientific scrutiny. Experimenters in this field believe that our memory, mind, personality, and soul will survive physical death.

For centuries, people have claimed that every living thing possesses an invisible (an astral or etheric) body that duplicates our physical body and contains our real "mind" (as distinct from our physical brain). Most interesting corroborative evidence for this claim was reported by Sheila Ostrander and Lynn Schroeder in their revolutionary *Psychic Discoveries behind the Iron Curtain* (1973).

These authors state that Soviet researchers using sensitive electronic equipment detected that all living things not only have a physical body made of atoms and molecules, but also a counterpart body of energy. They photographed it and called it the *biological plasma body*. Interestingly, Soviet researchers corroborate the centuries-old claim that if a person loses a limb, for example, the counterpart body remains whole—a kind of "ghost" of the missing limb.[31]

The out-of-body experience (OBE). The OBE is currently one of the most popular psychic research topics. This phenomenon is a powerful and consistent argument for survival after death. More particularly, the OBE continues to add to the voluminous evidence that the indestructible mind is independent of and

---

30 Crookes, 1874, p. 17.
31 Ostrander and Schroeder, 1973, p. 223.

separate from the physical brain. At all times, the OBE must be seen with other evidence for the afterlife.

The OBE happens when a person's duplicate invisible body (the astral or etheric body) leaves the physical body with full consciousness. Most people cannot control this event. One who experiences an OBE does not have to be ill or near death. Fenni Bey from Ordu (northern Turkey), who fought at the Madina front during the First World War, relates:

> We were under siege in Madina. I was unable to communicate with my family in Istanbul. One night in a dream I saw fire and smoke in my house. In the morning I sent for one of my privates who was known for his paranormal capacity. I told him to go into a trance, travel to my house (I told him where it was situated) and describe what he saw. He did what I told him and began to describe: "I have reached the house, I have knocked on the door and an old woman in a headscarf has come out with a child in her arms." I told the private to ask the woman if there was anything wrong in the house? He related to me: "She says your wife died yesterday."

Those who have had an OBE usually accept survival after death. They know they return to their physical body because their invisible duplicate body remains connected to it by a silver cord. When this cord is irretrievably severed, the invisible body survives in the afterlife.

The OBE is historical and has been reported from all over the world for over 20 centuries. For example:

- Ancient Egyptians described the OBE and the astral body as *ba*.
- Mithraic mystery initiation rites called for OBEs.
- Plato recalled the OBE of Er in his *Republic.*
- Socrates, Pliny, and Plotonius described OBEs. Plotonius wrote of being lifted out of his body on many occasions.
- Plutarch described an OBE that occurred to Aridanaeus in 79 CE.
- *The Tibetan Book of the Dead* describes a duplicate body, called a *bardo body*, that leaves the body.
- Mahayana Buddhism acknowledges the existence of a duplicate body.
- Ancient Chinese claimed they could experience an OBE after meditation.
- Some tribal shamans say that they can attain an OBE *at will*. North American Indians say some do have the necessary skills.

- Early missionaries in Africa and America were stunned that native tribes could have detailed knowledge of everything happening within a radius of hundreds of miles.[32]
- There are volumes of information about OBEs, including that gathered by American and Soviet researchers for military aims. Major David Morehouse writes:

> The secret is out: remote viewing (out-of-body experience) exists, it works, it has been tested, proven and used in intelligence for over two decades. The recent (US) government admissions concerning the use of psychic warfare are crucial, irrefutable testimony that what I have said here is the truth ...

The near death experience (NDE). Dr. Peter Fenwick, the most authoritative specialist on NDE in Britain, writes:

> There seems little doubt that NDEs occur in all cultures and have occurred at all times through recorded history ... The NDE happens to young and old, to people from all walks of life, to those whose life has a spiritual dimension and to those who profess no faith at all ... there are many examples of people who have a NDE at a time when they did not even know that such a phenomenon existed.

The NDE is a powerful argument for the existence of an afterlife. As medical advances bring more and more people back from the brink of clinical death, many recount an intense and profoundly meaningful experience in which they seem to be alive and functioning outside their body. For many, such an experience is very powerful, emotional, and spiritual.

Evidence for the NDE is consistent, overwhelming, and exoteric (experienced by the many). The experiential evidence is consistent with other experiential evidence for psychic phenomena, including the OBE. Although some skeptics refuse to believe in NDEs, more informed and the more formally educated skeptics now acknowledge that NDEs exist. The arena of dispute now is what it means.

Psychics say that in a crisis situation, where death is (or is perceived to be) almost inevitable, the astral or etheric body leaves the physical body and experiences the first stages of the afterlife. When death does not occur, it returns.

---

32 See Inglis, 1977, pp. 30-35.

Apparitions are consistent with the argument that we survive physical death. Objective evidence for apparitions is provided by case studies and laboratory-induced apparitions. Many such cases involve recently deceased people appearing to one or more loved ones to announce their deaths, which were usually unexpected and later confirmed to have occurred immediately before the apparition.

Throughout the twentieth century, books on the observations of doctors and nurses treating dying patients were published. Sir William Barrett, Professor of Physics at Dublin's Royal College of Science, published Deathbed Visions in 1926. In it he noted that at the moment of death, people often see at their bedside a friend or relative whom they thought was still living. When such cases were investigated, it was discovered that these people, unknown to those who saw them, had really died. Also, dying children often expressed surprise that the angels they saw waiting for them did not have wings.

In the 1960s, Dr Karlis Osis of the American Society for Psychical Research did a pilot study of deathbed visions. His work, later verified across several different cultures, reveals:

- The most common type of vision was of people who had died before them.
- Bedside visions usually lasted 5 minutes or less.
- Dying patients stated that the visitor had come to take them away.
- Belief in the afterlife has no significance on the frequency or kind of apparition seen.
- The majority of patients in the study had not received hallucination-inducing drugs.

In conclusion, such psychic phenomena as EVP, ITC, NDE, OBE, apparitions, and many others show conclusively that an afterlife does exist.

All messages received from higher intelligences in the Hereafter repeatedly inform us that, (succinctly put):

- We survive physical death, irrespective of our beliefs.
- At the point of death, we take our mind and all its experiences, our character, and our etheric/astral (spirit) body and leave our physical body. Our spirit body remains connected to our physical body as long as the silver cord is not severed. Death occurs when it is severed.
- Some dying people find it easy to leave the physical body, while others need help. Some very materialistic people will have a very heavy duplicate body, and will find it difficult to separate the two.

- Atheists, agnostics, and others may be prevented from passing on to higher spheres. Their beliefs, actions, and motivations will be important.
- Loved ones from the afterlife, recently arrived and others, can visit those who are still alive.
- The afterlife's life of beauty, peace, light, and love that awaits good people is unimaginable.
- One can learn spiritual lessons in the afterlife and progress to higher, more beautiful spheres.
- All physical, mental, and other disabilities will disappear for those people who lived good lives.
- Evil people are either left alone or will be met by others with the same very low vibrations and spiritual attainments. They will be attracted to the darker, lower spheres.
- Some people make a much better transition to the afterlife than others. In other words, the more knowledge and belief we have about the afterlife, the easier the transition.
- "You will reap what you sow" is the recognized universal spiritual law.
- Every thought, word, and deed is recorded, and you will be held accountable.
- Those in the higher spheres will be able to recall and see any event that happened while they were alive. They will see it three-dimensionally.
- Those who consistently abuse and harass others will face their victims before severe retribution. Cruelty, whether mental or physical and whether directed against humans or animals, will be accounted for. It can never be justified.

All this "scientific" evidence and the results obtained complies with what Said Nursi writes:

> Under the attacks of seductive and deceiving modern amusements and fancies, a group of young people sought help in order to save themselves from the punishment in the Hereafter. I said to them: Death is inevitable and, whether willingly or unwillingly, everyone will enter the grave. Apart from the following three ways, there is no other way of entering into it:
>
> *The first way:* For the believers, the grave is the door to a world exceedingly more beautiful than this one.

The second way: For those who confirm the next life but follow the way of dissipation and misguidance, it is the door to a solitary imprisonment, a jail, where they will be separated from all their loved ones. Since they do not practice their belief, that is exactly how they will be punished.

The third way: For the unbelievers and the misguided who do not believe in the Hereafter, it is the door to eternal "execution." That is, it is the gallows on which both they and their (unbelieving) comrades will be executed as an eternal punishment. Since they believe death to be an execution with no resurrection, they will find it as they believe it to be.

The appointed hour is secret. Death may come at any time to cut off anyone, without differentiating between young and old. In the face of such an awesome reality, people will search, as a matter of utmost urgency and concern, how to deliver themselves from an eternal punishment and an unending imprisonment, and how to change the door of the grave into a door opening onto a permanent world of light and eternal happiness.

Death will be experienced in these three ways. This has been reported by 124,000 truthful reporters—the Prophets, in whose hands are signs of truthfulness (miracles). Their report has been confirmed by countless saints relying on their discernment, vision, and intuition. Also, innumerable painstaking, truth-seeking scholars have proved it rationally with their decisive proofs at the level of "certainty depending on established knowledge." All these groups agree that only belief in God and obedience to Him [including, naturally, observing the rights of the created] can save people from eternal punishment and imprisonment, and make of the grave a way to eternal happiness.

If only one reliable reporter had warned that a particular way carried a 1 percent risk of the traveler perishing on it, you would lose your appetite for that way because of your resulting distress and fear. However, countless truthful, authoritative reporters (Prophets, saints, and verifying scholars) have warned us, based upon demonstrable proofs of their truth, that misguidance and dissipation carry a 100 percent risk of death and eternal punishment. By contrast, belief and worship remove both gallows and imprisonment, and change the grave into a door opening onto an eternal treasury, a palace of lasting happiness. In the face of such an extraordinary, awesome, and mighty warning, how can those of us who claim to believe and worship, but do not really do so, overcome the anxieties that come from waiting for our trip to those gallows, even if we had owned the world?

Seeing that old age, illness, misfortune, and numerous instances of death everywhere in the world open up that pain and remind us of it, even if the people of misguidance and dissipation seemingly enjoy innumerable kinds of pleasure and delight, they are most certainly in a hellish state of spiritual torment, albeit a profound stupor of heedlessness makes them temporarily insensible to it.

Since the grave is the door to an eternal treasury and endless happiness for obedient believers, and since, by reason of the "belief coupon," a ticket from the allocations of Destiny for billions worth of gold and diamonds has come up for them, they constantly expect the invitation, "Come and collect your ticket" with a secure, profound pleasure and spiritual delight. This pleasure is such that if it were to take on the material form of a seed, it would grow into a private paradise.

So, you unfortunate people who are addicted to worldly pleasures and, troubled about your future, struggle to secure it and your lives! If you want pleasure, delight, happiness, and ease in this world, be content with what is religiously lawful. That suffices for your enjoyment. In each forbidden pleasure lies a thousand pains. If the events of the future—for example, of 50 years hence—were shown in the cinema in the same way that they now show past events, those who are now leading a dissipated life would weep with horror and disgust at the things with which they entertain themselves.

Those who wish to be permanently, eternally happy in this world and the next should follow the instruction of Muhammad, upon him be peace and blessings, on the firm ground of belief.

Human nature. Humanity is a unique part of creation, for God placed within each individual some aspect of all that exists in the universe. Our mental and spiritual faculties cause us to represent angelic and other spiritual worlds (world of symbols or immaterial forms). Our innate capacity to learn and our (limited) free will gives us the potential to excel angels. Our physical bodies cause us to represent plants and animals. Although we are contained in time and space, our spiritual faculties and such other powers as imagination make it possible to transcend them.

We also have supreme importance. We dominate the Earth, most of its creatures, and subordinate and gather around us almost all living things. We order, display, and ornament created objects according to our needs and desires; catalogue and classify everything in all its wonderful variety and each species in its own place; our way of doing so attracts the gaze of other people and jinn, the appreciative regard of the dwellers of the Heavens and of the universe, even the admiring glance of the Master of the universe.

We use our arts and sciences to display our position as the purpose behind the universe's creation. We show that we are the great consequence and supreme fruit of creation, and that we act as God's vicegerents. We are given respite in this life and our punishment is postponed, despite our rebellion and disbelief. Due to the services we perform, we are granted a temporary reprieve and the Almighty's assistance.

Each of us is equal in value and comprehensiveness to an entire animate species, for our intellect has endowed us with comprehensive aspirations and ideas that encompass the past and future. All other animate species have the following characteristics: the nature of each member is particular and its value is restricted to itself; their view is restricted, their qualities are limited, and their pleasure and pain are instantaneous.

On the contrary, we have a sublime nature and the greatest value, our perfection is limitless, and our spiritual pleasures and pains are more permanent. Thus we can conclude that the resurrection experienced by non-human species suggest that each one of us will be resurrected completely on the Day of Judgment.

Our human conscience, our conscious nature, indicates eternal happiness. Whoever listens to it will hear it pronouncing eternity over and over again. The whole universe could not compensate us for our lack of eternity. We have an innate longing for eternity, as we were created for it. Our innate, ardent, irremovable, and persistent love of eternity; longing for immortality; and desire for permanence prove that there is an eternal hereafter (including a realm of happiness) after this transient world.

If we could choose between eternal life with severe hardship and eternal non-existence after a short yet luxurious life, most probably we would prefer the first option. We would even prefer eternal existence in Hell to eternal non-existence. God, the All-Merciful and All-Wise, did not condemn us to eternal non-existence, or give us a desire for eternity so that we would suffer from a heartfelt desire that we could not satisfy. So Divine Wisdom requires the existence of an eternal world in which we will live eternally.

This world cannot properly judge our worth. Although our bodies are small, our mental and spiritual faculties allow us to embrace the universe. Our acts do not relate only to the visible world, and cannot be restricted by time and space. Our nature is so universal that even the acts of the first human being affects the life and character of the last, on the whole of existence. The materialists' restriction of humanity to a short-lived and spatially limited physical entity shows a complete lack of understanding and appreciation of what each human being really is.

The scales of this world cannot weigh the following:

- The Prophets' intellectual and spiritual value and achievements.
- The destruction caused by such monsters as Pharaoh, Hitler, Stalin, and the like.
- The true value of sincere belief and moral qualities.

How can you reward a martyr who has sacrificed everything for the sake of God, or for others, or for such universal human values as justice and truthfulness? How can you reward believing scientists who dedicate their lives to serving humanity by inventing something that will benefit everyone until the end of time? Only the scales of the other world, scales that can weigh an atom's weight of good or evil, can perform this task properly and with full justice, for:

> We set up a just balance for the Day of Resurrection. Thus, no soul will be treated unjustly. Even though it be the weight of one mustard seed, We shall bring it forth to be weighed; and Our reckoning will suffice. (21:47)

Even if there were no Resurrection, the necessity of weighing our deeds alone would require an infinitely just and sensitive balance to be set up.

As this world is not exactly propitious for a complete development of human potentialities, we are destined to achieve realization in another world. Our comprehensive essence means that we are bound for eternity. Our essentially sublime nature allows us to engage in both good and evil. As order and discipline are essential, we cannot be left to ourselves or condemned to eternal annihilation. Hell is waiting for us with a wide-open mouth; Paradise is expecting us with open arms.

CHAPTER 4
THE SPIRIT

The Spirit[33]

S cience is not yet fully ready to accept the spirit's existence. However, this does not rule out the existence of subdivisions within a world, such as the plant, animal, and human worlds, or the existence of other worlds within the universe. Our visible, material world addresses our senses. From the tiniest particles to galaxies, this is where God Almighty gives life, fashions, renews, changes, and makes to die. Science concerns itself with the phenomena of this world.

Above this world is the immaterial world of Divine Laws or Commands. To gain some knowledge of it, consider how a book, a tree, or a person comes into existence. The main part of a book's existence is its meaning. It cannot exist if it has no meaning, regardless of how excellent our printing press is or how much paper we have. Or, consider what stimulates a seed to germinate underground and grow into a tree: the essence of life and the law of germination and growth with which it is endowed. We can see it germinate and become a tree. Without this there would be no plants, for the essence of life and the laws of germination and growth, although invisible or unobservable, govern a living thing's birth and growth.

Similarly, menstruation prepares a woman's womb every month for insemination. This process is dictated by a (biological) law. Out of millions of sperms heading for the womb, one reaches the ovum to fertilize it. After this, menstruation stops until birth. This is another process governed by another (biological) law. The embryo's development into a new individual through many stages is a third process governed by other (biological or embryological) laws.

We deduce the existence of such laws from the almost never-changing repetition of these processes. Likewise, by observing the (natural) phenomena around us, we also deduce the existence of many other laws like gravitation, repulsion, and the freezing or vaporization of water.

The spirit is also a law. But unlike the others, it is a living, conscious, and light-giving law furnished with external or sensible existence. It has the potential to achieve universality. Even natural laws, considerably weak when compared to the spirit, have stability and permanence. One can recognize that all

---

33 Fethullah Gülen, *The Essentials of the Islamic Faith*, Chapter 4.

kinds of existence, although subject to change, possess a permanent dimension that remains unaltered through all stages of life.

The body is ephemeral, whereas the spirit inhabiting it is permanent. Any change in the body or its constituent elements does not affect the spirit. The spirit changes or renews its garment (its body) each year. When it strips off this garment for the last time (death), the spirit's permanence is not affected and its essential nature is not spoiled, for the body subsists through the spirit, not the spirit through the body. We can even say that the body, rather than being the spirit's cover, is its dwelling place. The spirit has a subtle cover, which can be called its ethereal envelope. When the body dies, the spirit leaves its dwelling place dressed in its subtle cover.

Each human being is simultaneously an individual and an entire species, for each individual has a comprehensive nature, a universal consciousness, and an all-embracing imagination. A law operating on humanity also applies to the individual.

The Majestic Creator has endowed each person with a sublime nature and caused him or her to be a comprehensive mirror through which all His Attributes and Names are reflected. He also has charged each of us with a universal duty of worship. So, each individual's spiritual reality remains alive forever, by Divine Permission, even though its form undergoes numerous changes.

From all of the above, we can conclude that the human spirit, which constitutes a person's conscious, living element, is eternal and has been made so by God's command and permission.

How can we establish the spirit's existence? Matter or anything in the material world is composed of atoms, which are made up of more minute particles. The spirit, however, is a simple entity and thus is not subject to disintegration. We cannot see it as we see a material thing; we know it through its manifestations in the material world. Although we accept its existence and observe its manifestations, we cannot know its nature. Our ignorance of something's nature, however, does not mean that it does not exist.

Although materialists attribute our intellectual faculties to our brains, studies on physic phenomena demonstrate that what we call mind is independent of and distinct from our physical brain. Very interesting corroborative evidence for this claim was reported by Ostrander and Schroeder.[34]

We see with our eyes. In other words, our eyes are simply instruments with which to see. The main center of sight is in the brain. However, the brain itself does not "see." You say: "I see," not "My brain sees." We see, hear, or sense things. But who is this "I"? Is it something composed of a brain, a heart, and other organs and limbs? Why can we not move when we die, although all our organs and limbs are there?

To draw an analogy, how does a factory work: by itself or by something we call electricity? Any defect or mistake in the factory that causes a disconnection between it and electricity can reduce a whole highly productive and invaluable factory to a heap of junk. Is this relation between the factory and electricity somehow comparable to that between the spirit and the body? When the body-spirit connection is broken at the time of death, the body is reduced to something that will soon begin to rot and decompose.

Of course, the spirit is not an electrical power. It is a conscious, powerful thing that can learn, think, sense, and reason. It is continually developing, usually in parallel with the body's physical development, as well as mentally and spiritually via learning, reflection, belief, and worship. The spirit also determines an individual's character, nature, or identity and so makes one unique. Although all human beings are substantially made from the same elements, they are all unique in their characters, natures, and features, right down to their fingerprints. It is one's spirit that determines this difference.

The spirit commands our inner faculties. All of creation acts according to its God-given primordial nature. This is why we observe a strict determinism in the universe's operation. What we call natural laws are really the names we give to how a creature exercises its God-given primordial nature through its behavior or attributes. The primordial nature of things does not "deceive." For example, God told the Earth to revolve on its axis and around the sun, and thus it must do so. A seed says in the tongue of its being or primordial nature: "I will germinate underground in proper conditions and grow into a plant," and it does what it says. Water declares that it freezes at 0°C and boils at 100°C, and does what it declares.

---

34 Sheila Ostrander and Lyn Schroeder, *PSI: Psychic Discoveries Behind the Iron Curtain*, Sphere Books, London: 1973.

Similarly, the human conscience, as long as it remains sound, does not lie. If it is not deluded by the carnal self or desires, it deeply feels God's existence and finds peace through belief in and worship of Him. Thus, the spirit directs or commands human conscience and all other human faculties. The spirit seeks the world from which it came, and yearns for its Creator. Unless it is stunted and spoiled with sins, it will find the Creator and, in Him, will attain true happiness.

The spirit has deep relations to the past and future. Animals have no conception of time, as their God-given primordial nature causes them to live only in the present. Human beings, however, are deeply influenced by the pain of past events and misfortunes, and are anxious about their future. This is because the human spirit is a conscious, sentient entity.

The spirit is never satisfied with this mortal, fleeting world. Our accomplishments, wealth, status or position, and the satisfaction of all worldly desires is never enough to make the spirit happy. Rather, worldly gains make it more dissatisfied and unhappy. It finds rest only in belief, worship, and remembrance of God.

Each person has a strong desire for eternity. This desire cannot come from the physical dimension, for in physical terms we are mortal, and the feeling of and desire for eternity cannot arise from that which is mortal. Rather, it originates in the eternal dimension of our existence: the spirit. It is the spirit that causes someone to sigh: "I am mortal, but I don't desire what is mortal. I am impotent, but I don't desire what is impotent. What I desire is an eternal beloved (who will never desert me), and I yearn for an eternal world."

The spirit establishes its connection with the material world through the body. The spirit is a simple entity issuing from the world of Divine Commands. In order to be manifested and function in this world, it needs material means. As the body cannot get in touch with the world of symbols or immaterial forms, the spirit can establish contact with this world only through the mediation of the heart, the brain, and other bodily organs and limbs.

As the spirit functions through the body's nerves, cells, and other elements, its relation can be severed if something happens to the body's system or organs. When this happens, the spirit can no longer control the affected part. If the spirit's contact with the entire body is somehow severed, the body dies. Although some meaningless movements can be seen in the hands or fingers if certain areas of the brain are stimulated, these movements resemble the confused, meaningless sounds produced by randomly pressing piano keys. Also, such movements are automatic bodily responses to any stimulation, and are due to the body's automatic workings. In other words, if the body has no spirit, it cannot produce meaningful movements.

Although such psychoanalysts like Freud have devised various explanations, dreams cannot be said to consist of the subconscious self's jumbled activities. Almost everyone has had one or more dreams that accurately foretold the future. Also, many scientific or technological discoveries are the result of "true" dreams. So, dreams point to the existence of something within the person that can see in a different way while the person is sleeping. This part is the spirit.

The spirit sees with the eyes, smells with the nose, hears with the ears and so on, but many people have demonstrated an ability to see with their fingers or the tips of their noses, and to smell with their heels.

The spirit determines one's facial features. The spirit manifests itself mainly on one's face, making it a window opening onto one's internal world. Through all its features, one's face discloses one's character. Psychologists assert that almost all one's movements, even coughing, reveal one's character. Reading one's face to discover one's character, abilities, and personality is known as physiognomy.

Bodily cells are continually renewed. Every day millions of cells die and are replaced. Biologists say that one's entire body is renewed every 6 months. And yet one's main facial features never change. This is how we recognize each other. The same is true of our fingerprints. Cell renewal, injury, or bruise cannot change our fingerprints. Such stability of our distinguishing features is due to our unique spirit.

The spirit receives moral, spiritual, and intellectual education, and causes character differences. The body continues to change until its death. This change takes the form of physical growth and development, which makes the body stronger and more perfect, until a certain point is reached. Then, growth stops and decay begins. However, a person can continue to grow intellectually or spiritually forever, stop at a certain point and change direction, or allow his or her intellectual and spiritual faculties to decay. In other words, one's moral, spiritual, and intellectual education does not depend on bodily changes.

Moral, spiritual, and intellectual differences also have nothing to do with physical structure. Every human being is composed of the same material. Why then are there moral and intellectual differences among them? What part receives moral and intellectual education, and what part is trained physically?

Does physical training have any relation to learning and moral and intellectual education? Can we say that the more physical training a person receives and the more developed one's body becomes, the more one develops in learning and morality?

If we cannot, why should we not accept the spirit's existence? How could we attribute learning and moral and intellectual education to some biochemical processes in the brain? Are those processes faster in some people than in others? Are some more developed intellectually because these processes are faster in them, or are they faster because some study and develop their intellects to a higher degree than others? What relation do such processes have with one's spiritual and moral education and development? How can we explain the facial differences caused by regular worship? Why do believers have more radiant faces than unbelievers and sinners?

Our bodies clearly change. However, our character, morality, and thinking do not change in parallel with our physical changes. How can we explain this, other than by admitting that the spirit is the center of thinking, feeling, choice, decision, and learning, and that it is the source of our differences of opinion, preferences, and character differences?

The spirit feels and believes or disbelieves. A human being has innumerable, complex feelings: love, hate, joy, grief, happiness, sadness, hope, desperation, ambition, imaginings, relief, boredom, and so on. Each person likes or dislikes, appreciates or disregards, fears or becomes timid, becomes encouraged and feels enthusiastic, repents, becomes excited, and longs. We have hundreds of words to express our feelings, and never experience the same feeling in exactly the same manner as someone else.

Moreover, a human being may reflect on surrounding events or the beauty in creation, and thereby develop intellectually. An individual can compare and reason, and then believe in the Creator of all things. Then through worship and following His Commandments, a person develops morally and spiritually and becomes a perfect human being. How can we explain all of these phenomena other than by admitting that each of us has a conscious spirit? Can we attribute them to chemical processes in the brain?

A person's real identity and personality lies in one's spirit. If we limit an individual to his or her physical body and attribute all of his or her movements to biochemical processes in the brain, how can we enforce any laws? Suppose a person is being tried for a murder he or she committed one year ago. The following scenario would be entirely logical:

-Judge: "When did you commit that crime?"

-Accused: "A year ago."

-Judge: "Since the murder was committed a year ago, the body of the accused has completely regenerated itself. This includes the trigger finger. Therefore the accused cannot be punished, for the body that committed the murder no longer exists."

The judge would have no option but to advise the jury to recommend acquittal, for the "new" person cannot be punished for what the "old" person did.

Given that such a situation would reduce existence to an absurdity, we must admit that each individual has a spirit. The main part of each individual is his or her spirit, which is alive and conscious, and which feels, thinks, believes, wills, and decides. It also commands the body, which is the instrument used by the spirit to put its decisions into action.

The spirit is the basis of human life. God acts in this world behind the veil of causes. However, there are many other worlds or realms, such as the world of ideas, symbols, immaterial forms, the inner dimensions of things, and spirits. In these worlds, God acts directly, and matter and causes are not operative. The spirit is breathed into the embryo directly, without the mediation of causes. It is a direct manifestation of the Divine Name the All-Living, and therefore the basis of human life. Like "natural" laws, which issue from the same realm from which the spirit is sent, the spirit is invisible and known through its manifestations.

In this world, matter is refined in favor of life. A lifeless body, regardless of size, is lonely, passive, and static. But life enables such a small creature as a bee to interact with almost the whole world, and causes it to go as far as saying: "This world is my garden; flowers are my business partners." The smaller a living body, the more active, astonishing, and powerful is its life. Compare a bee, a fly, or a micro-organism with an elephant. The more refined matter is, the more active and powerful is its body. For example, burning wood produces flames and carbon, heated water vaporizes, and electrical energy exists in the atomic or subatomic world. We cannot see it, but we are aware of its power through its manifestations.

Thus, existence is not limited only to this visible, material world. Rather, this world is only the apparent, mutable, and unstable dimension of existence. Behind it lies the pure invisible dimension, which uses matter to be seen and known. This is the dimension to which the spirit belongs. Therefore, our spirits are pure and invisible.

The spirit has its own cover or envelope. The body is not the spirit's cover. Rather, the spirit has its own cover or envelope. When it leaves the body at death, it puts on this cover, which is like a "negative" of the body and is known as the astral or ethereal body. Such images can be captured and made visible through special photographic techniques, as discussed earlier. Even amputated limbs can be seen.

THE CRY OF A HEART DISSATISFIED WITH THE PASSING WORLD IN YEARNING FOR ETERNITY[35]

Despite all my needs and innate weakness, destitution and help-lessness, and while being in a wretched state due to the terrors and loneliness coming from the six directions, I have infinite desires and ambitions extending to eternity, and inscribed on the page of my being by the Pen of Power and embedded in my nature.

Indeed, whatever there is in the universe, there are samples of it in my being. I am connected with all of them. I work for them.

The sphere of need is as extensive as the eye reaches. In fact, wherever the imagination goes, the sphere of need extends that far. Rather, what-ever I do not possess, I am in need of it. What I do not possess is without limits, whereas the extent of my power is as narrow as my arm reaches. This means that my wants and needs are of infinite quantity, whereas my capital is as little and insignificant as an atom.

So, what does that insignificant willpower signify in the face of these infinite needs that can only be obtained with millions? They cannot be satisfied by it. Therefore, I should search for another solution.

The solution is this: Never relying on one's own power, to submit oneself to the Divine Will and seek refuge in His Power in adherence to the reality of trusting in Him. "O Master! Since this is the way of salvation, I take refuge in You and abandon my ego. So that Your grace may help and support me out of compassion for my impotence and

---

35 Said Nursi, *The Words*, "17th Word."

weakness, and Your Mercy may take pity on me because of my want and need and be a support for me, and open its door to me."

Whoever finds the boundless sea of Mercy does not rely on their own power any more than on a drop from the water seen in a mirage. Whoever resorts to Mercy does not resort to their will.

Alas! We have been deceived. We thought the worldly life is constant, and lost it thoroughly because of this thought. Indeed, this passing life is but a sleep; it has passed like a dream. This unbounded life too, flies like the wind.

Those who rely on themselves and suppose that they will live forever will certainly die. They advance toward death speedily. The world too, which is humanity's house, falls into the darkness of annihilation. Ambitions are time-bound, but pain endures in the spirit.

Since this is the reality, come, O my wretched soul, which is fond of living and desirous of a long life, which loves the world deeply and is afflicted with countless ambitions and pains! Awaken and come to your senses! Consider that while the firefly relies on its own dim light and always remains in the boundless darkness of the night, the honeybee finds the sun of daytime and observes its friends, the flowers, gilded with the sunlight because it does not rely on itself.

In just the same way, if you rely on yourself and your being, your own self-confidence, you will be like the firefly. But if you dedicate yourself, your transient being and your body in a self-sacrificing way in the way of the Creator Who gave it to you, then you will find, like the honeybee, an endless life of being. Dedicate it, for your being, your body, is a Divine trust to you.

Also, it is the Creator's property; He gave it to you. So use it in His way unhesitatingly and without placing anybody under obligation. Sacrifice it so that it will gain permanence, for a negation negated is an affirmation. Thus, if our non-being is negated (in favor of Being), our being finds true existence.

The All-Munificent Creator "buys" His own property from you. In return, He gives you a high price like Paradise. Also, He looks after it well for you, and increases its value. He will return it to you in a form both perfected and made permanent. So, O my soul, do not wait! Do this business which is profitable in many respects, and, as well as being saved from many losses, make a fivefold profit in a single transaction.

***

The verse, "I love not things that set," which was uttered by the Prophet Abraham, upon him be peace, and announces the decay of the universe, made me weep. The eyes of my heart wept for it and poured bitter tears. As the eyes of the heart wept, each teardrop was so bitterly sad that it caused others to fall, as though the tears themselves were weeping. Those tears make up the lines that follow.

The tears are like a sort of commentary on some words of a wise Prophet contained in the Word of God: the Qur'an.

A beloved who disappears by declining or setting is not beautiful, for one that is doomed to decline cannot be truly beautiful. It is not, nor should it be, loved in the heart for the heart is created for eternal love and is the mirror of the Eternally-Besought-of-All.

A desired one who is doomed to disappear below the horizon is not worthy of the heart's attachment or the mind's preoccupation. It cannot be the object of desires, and is not worthy of being regretted. So why should the heart adore such a one and be attached to it? I neither seek nor desire anything mortal. For I am myself mortal, and I do not desire one who is mortal. What have I do with any such?

A worshipped one buried in decay—I do not invoke such a one, nor seek refuge with it. For one that is itself powerless cannot cure for my endless pain, nor can it solve my infinitely deep wounds. How can one who cannot save itself from decay be an object of worship?

The mind that is obsessed with appearances wails despairingly on seeing the decay of the things it adores in this universe of upheavals, while the spirit, which seeks an eternal beloved, also wails, saying: "I love not the things that set. I do not want, I do not desire, separation, and I cannot endure it."

Meetings followed immediately by separation are not worth troubling about; they are not worthy of being longed for especially. For just as the disappearance of pleasure is pain, imagining it is pain also. The works of lovers, namely, poetry on metaphorical love (love for the opposite sex) are all lamentations caused by the pain arising from imagining this disappearance. If you were to condense the spirit of all such poetry, from each would flow this lament.

It is because of the pain and tribulation coming from those meetings doomed to end and those painful metaphorical loves that my heart cries out and, like Abraham, says: "I love not the things that set!"

If you desire permanence in this transient world, permanence is born out of transience. Annihilate yourself with regard to your carnal, evil-commanding soul, so that you may gain permanence.

Free yourself of bad morals, which are the basis of worldly adoration, and realize self-annihilation. Sacrifice the goods and property that are in your disposal in the way of the True Beloved. See the end of beings, which marks extinction. The way leading from this world to permanence passes through self-annihilation.

The human mind, which is absorbed in causality, laments in bewilderment over the upheavals caused by the world's decay. The conscience, which desires true existence, like Abraham, wails: "I love not the things that set." It severs the connection with metaphorical beloveds and decaying beings, and is attached to the Truly Existent One, the Eternal Beloved.

O my mean soul! Know that the world and all beings are certainly mortal, but you may find a way leading to the Permanent Being in each mortal thing. You may discern two gleams, two mysteries, of the manifestations of the Undying Beloved's Grace, on condition that you sacrifice your mortal being.

In each bounty, the act of bestowing is discerned and the favor of the Most Merciful perceived. If you discern the act of bestowing through the thing bestowed, you will find the Bestower. Also, each work of the Eternally-Besought-of-All points out the All-Majestic Maker's Names like a missive. If you understand the meaning through the inscription, you will find by means of the Names the One called by those Names. Since you can find out the kernel, the essence, of these transient things, obtain it. You can throw away without pity their meaningless shells, their outer coverings, into the flood of mortality.

Indeed, in the universe everything is a word of embodied meaning and shows many of the All-Majestic Maker's Names. Since beings are words, words of Divine Power, understand their meanings and place them in your heart. Fearlessly cast the letters left without meaning into the wind of transience. After they are gone, do not concern and occupy yourself with them any more.

The worldly mind, preoccupied with appearances and whose capital consists of only knowledge of the material world, cries out in bewilderment and frustration, as its chains of thought finally end in nothingness and non-existence. It seeks a true way leading to truth. Since the heart has withdrawn from those that set and are mortal, since the heart has abandoned the deceiving beloveds, and since the conscience has turned away from transitory beings, you too, my wretched soul, seek help in "I love not the things that set" and be saved.

See how well Mawlana Jami expressed it, intoxicated with the "wine" of love as if created from love:

> Want only One (the rest are not worth wanting)
> Call One (the others will not come to your help)
> Seek One (the others are not worth seeking)
> See and follow One (the others are not seen all
> the time; they become invisible
> behind the veil of mortality)
>
> Know One (knowledge other than that which adds to
> your knowledge of Him is of no benefit)
> Mention One (words not concerning Him may be considered
> without benefit and useless).

O Jami, I admit that you spoke the truth absolutely. The True Beloved, the True Sought One, the True Desired One, and the True Object of Worship is He alone. In the mighty circle for the remembrance and recitation of God's Names, this universe, together with all its beings in various tongues and different tones declares: There is no deity but God, and testifies to Divine Oneness. It salves the wound caused by those that set, and, in place of all the deceiving beloveds, points to the Undying Beloved.

CHAPTER 5
THEOLOGICAL AND QUR'ANIC
ARGUMENTS

THEOLOGICAL AND QUR'ANIC
ARGUMENTS[36]

E very village has its headman, every needle a manufacturer, and every letter an author. How can this universe, so extremely well-ordered a realm, not have a creator and ruler? Knowing this Ruler with His Essential Qualities, Attributes, and Names and believing in Him is a wide door opening on the Resurrection and the afterlife.

THEOLOGICAL ARGUMENTS

Belief in God requires belief in the afterlife for the following reasons:

God's being an All-Majestic, Eternal Master requires it. The universe displays a strict, well-established order that no being can destroy. Every being, except those in conscious rebellion, pays great attention to their duties. They do not transgress their bounds, and as a result no disorder in the universe, now several billion years old, has ever appeared. The greatest conscious beings—Prophets and saints—engage in the most modest and obedient service with joy and zeal, as well as with fear and awe, for every created item obeys God's command like an obedient soldier.

The Divine Majesty seen in the seasonal changes, the planets' sublime orbits, all things' orderliness, the Earth's creation as humanity's cradle and the sun as humanity's lamp, and such vast transformations as reviving and adorning the dry, dead Earth—all show that a sublime Mastership and majestic Sovereignty rules from behind the veil of what is seen.

That infinite, glorious Sovereignty requires subjects worthy of itself and a fitting vehicle for its manifestation. But reflecting upon this temporary world, we see that its most important inhabitants, those blessed with the most comprehensive functions, are gathered here only for a while and in a wretched state. The hostel is filled and emptied daily, for it is only a temporary arena of trial and testing in service. All of the Sovereign's subjects stay only for a few moments to look over, like would-be buyers, the samples of precious gifts bestowed by the Majestic Maker. Then they depart, while the show continues

---

36 ibid, "10th Word" and "29th Word"; Fethullah Gülen, *The Essentials of the Islamic Faith*, Chapter 4.

to change by the minute. Whoever departs never returns, and whoever comes eventually departs.

Given this, would God, Majestic and Eternal, focus Himself entirely upon these transient beings and not create a permanent sphere to manifest eternally all His Attributes and Names? Would the glory of God's being a sovereign, all-sustaining Master allow Him to create a universe with lofty aims and purposes, but one devoid of any reward for those believers who seek, by faith and worship, to act in accordance with the universe's order and to satisfy those aims and purposes? Could He create one devoid of any punishment for those who reject His purposes and seek to destroy the order?

No! This state of affairs argues that behind and beyond this temporary world lies a permanent, eternal abode that manifests fully the everlasting Sovereignty of God—palaces, gardens, treasure houses stocked with pure and perfect originals of the copies we see in this world. We strive here for what awaits us there. We labor here and are rewarded there. Bliss awaits each individual—if they are not among the losers—according to his or her capacity. We affirm that an Eternal Sovereignty cannot focus exclusively upon a realm whose transience makes it wretched.

God's being the All-Munificent and All-Merciful requires it. Reflect upon this: Are not all animate beings given appropriate sustenance? The weakest and most powerless receive the best sustenance. The more needy and helpless a creature is, the better it is nourished. For example, during the first stages of life, we are nourished in the best way and without effort. As we become adults aware of our personal strength and willpower, we begin to meet their needs with great difficulty. But fruit-worms live on the best food and quite easily, and immobile plants take their food ready and without effort.

In spring, trees are dressed in silk-like finery, covered in blossoms and fruits as if bejeweled, and bear the choicest fruits on their branches, stretched out like the hands of a generous person who takes great pleasure in favoring others. We receive sweet, wholesome honey from a stinging insect; we can dress in the finest, softest cloth woven by handless silkworms; and within the tiniest seeds are stored great treasures of mercy for us. Again, the way all vegetable, animal, and human mothers tenderly and compassionately nurture the growth of their helpless infants with milk manifests an all-embracing mercy.

These and many other examples of bountiful largesse and noble magnanimity show that there is One absolutely Merciful and Munificent Who rules, sustains, or maintains all creatures. The Majestic Master and Ruler of this world has infinite munificence and mercy.

As God is eternal, so are His Mercy and Munificence. An Eternal One manifests Himself eternally, and requires the existence of eternal beings. His eternal Mercy and Munificence demand eternal manifestation, and therefore eternal beings on whom to confer His bounties eternally. The present, material world is subject to perishing, for the daily deaths of millions of living creatures and the extinction of numerous lives indicates this world's final, overall death. In this impermanent world, hardly any of this Attribute is established and manifested. Human beings, in particular, cannot gratify all of their desires and appetites. Such qualities as youth, beauty, and strength, upon which we set our hearts, desert us without notice and leave great sorrow and grief.

Human life is very short and the pleasures derived from the results of Divine Mercy disappear when tasted. No one departs from this world fully satisfied. If there were no eternal life in which we will taste the results of this Mercy and receive greater pleasure, this Mercy would be a source of continuous lament and regret. It would be a pain, even an insult and a mockery, to no longer nourish those needy ones who have tasted such nourishment already. In the absence of an eternal life in which we can gratify our desires eternally, all God-given bounties and blessings would become pain and sorrow.

For a blessing to be real, it must be constant. An irreversible death or disappearance would turn compassion into torment, love into separation, blessing into curse, reason into wretchedness, and pleasure into pain, all of which cause the Divine Mercy to vanish. Thus, there must be a blessed, eternal realm more fitting to God's eternal, infinite Munificence and Mercy or where they will be seen in all their perfection.

God's being the All-Generous and All-Gracious requires it. A saint once asked the 'Abbasid caliph Harun al-Rashid: "If you desperately needed a glass of water, would you abandon your kingdom in return for it?" The caliph said that he would. The saint asked: "If you could not discharge it from your body, would you give up kingdom in order to do so?" The caliph said that he would. The saint concluded: "Then all of your wealth and kingdom consist of a glass of water."

The face of the world is adorned with so many objects of grace: the sun and moon are its lamps, and its surface teems with the finest varieties of sustenance, an overflowing feast of plenty, trees bearing fruits like so many dishes and renewed several times each season. Whatever we need is provided for almost nothing. The more necessary a thing is, the more abundant and cheaper it is in nature. What we need the most is air, which is free. Then comes water, which is almost free. We have nothing to do with its formation. Next come heat and light, which the sun sends for nothing. The other bounties with which we are blessed are extremely cheap, and our effort to procure them is minute.

All of this shows the existence of unlimited generosity and liberality and unequaled eternal grace. However, if these bounties were not given to us eternally and in a much better fashion, fear of death would change them into poison whenever we consumed even a morsel of them.

As God is eternal, with all His Names and Attributes and without changing His blessings into pain because of fear of death, He makes death a changing of worlds, a discharge from worldly duties, an invitation and passport to the eternal abode He has prepared for us. Out of His eternal Liberality, Generosity, and Grace, which require an abode of blissful repose that is both everlasting and contains all desirable objects, He will provide us eternally and without any effort on our part with ever better forms of the bounties He bestows on us here. Just as the cessation of pain is a sort of pleasure, the cessation of pleasure is a sort of pain. This is something that unlimited generosity cannot countenance.

God's being the All-Pitying and Caring requires it. Divine Pity and Caring heals wounds, wounded hearts, and feelings. Without them, you could not stop a bleeding wound. Divine Pity and Caring cause a patient to recover, the pangs of separation to stop, and change pain and sorrow into joy and pleasure. They help humanity and animals in all stages of their lives, especially before and after birth. In their embryonic stages, their mothers' wombs are well-protected homes in which they are nourished directly and effortlessly. After their births, Divine Pity and Caring send them breast-milk, the best possible food. Each parent's feelings of pity and caring are a single manifestation of their Divine originals.

Divine Pity and Caring encompass the universe; but we encounter in the world numerous unhealed wounds and wounded feelings, and cases of incurable illness, hunger, thirst, and poverty. As is the case with Divine Mercy and Munificence, the material world cannot receive all the manifestations of Divine Pity and Caring. Our inability to do so, in addition to human injustice and misuse of their inborn abilities, intervenes between beings and the manifestations of the Divine Pity and Caring. Above all, death is the fate of all living beings, and nothing but belief in another, eternal world can stop the sorrows it arouses in hearts.

God's Messenger once was sitting in the mosque when some prisoners of war were brought to him. A woman anxiously looking for someone caught his attention. She took each boy she saw to her bosom and then left him. She must have been looking for her son. At last she found him and, embracing him, pressed him to her bosom and caressed him with great affection. This caused the Messenger to burst into tears. Pointing to her, he asked his Companions: "Do you see that woman? Does she throw that child in her arms into Hell?" "No," the Companions answered, and the Messenger said: "God is much more compassionate than that woman. He does not throw His servants into Hell [unless the servants absolutely deserve it]." In the other world, Divine Pity and Caring will be manifested fully, without any intervention, sorrow, or pain.

God's being the All-Wise and All-Just requires it. The One Who administers this world does so in accordance with infinite wisdom. This is seen in how the use and benefit of all things is manifested. Have you not seen how many wise purposes are served by each limb, bone, and vein in a human body, by each brain cell and every particle therein? The purposes are as numerous as the fruits of a tree, which confirms that all is arranged in accordance with infinite wisdom. A further proof is the absolute orderliness with which everything has been fashioned.

The miniaturization of the whole, exact program of a beautiful flower's growth in a tiny seed, making by the Pen of Destiny a tree's seed the index of its life history and all its parts, show that an absolute wisdom moves that Pen. The perfection of the subtle artistry in all things proves the impress of an infinitely Wise Artist. The inclusion within the small human body of an index of all being, of the keys to all the treasuries of Mercy, and of the mirrors to all the Divine Names, further demonstrates the Wisdom within that infinitely subtle artistry. Is it conceivable that the Wisdom that so permeates the workings of Mastership would not wish to favor eternally those who seek refuge in that Mastership's protection and who are faithfully obedient?

As God is the All-Wise Who acts in absolute wisdom, He is also the All-Just Who puts everything where it must be. He acts in absolute balance and with the most precise measure, and gives everything its due. Do you need convincing that all things are done with justice and balance? Consider these facts: All things are given being and form, and then placed according to a precise equilibrium and measure; all things receive tall the necessities of their being and the requirements of life in the most fitting form, and according to their nature; and every petition and plea is voiced in the tongue of disposition, of natural need or necessity. All of these show infinite justice and wisdom.

Could the justice and wisdom that hasten to provide the smallest of creation (with what it needs) fail to provide the greatest need of humanity, the greatest of creatures, namely immortality? Could it fail to respond to humanity's greatest plea and cry for help, or that it would not preserve the dignity of God's being Master by granting the dues of His servants?

Actually, God's Names and Attributes are all absolute and eternal. As He is absolutely and eternally Merciful, Relenting, and Forgiving, so is He absolutely and eternally Mighty, Just, and Dignified. *Although His Mercy embraces all things* (7:156) and, as stated in a hadith, exceeds His wrath, some people commit such great crimes and sins that their due can only be severe punishment. Besides, despite the Divine declaration that *whoever kills a human being unjustly has killed all of humanity* (5:32), especially now when might is right, thousands of innocent people are killed daily, many others are wronged and deprived of their basic human rights, and many heinous sins and injustices go unpunished.

Death takes the oppressed and the oppressor, the innocent and the guilty, the sinless and the sinful. Small crimes are judged in small courts, great crimes are referred to supreme tribunals, and such great crimes and sins as unbelief, associating partners with God, murder, and oppression are postponed until God will judge them with His absolute Justice.

One day those who thanked God, acted justly, and lived innocent lives will be welcomed with: *Eat and drink to your hearts content because of what you did in days gone by* (69:24) and *Peace be upon you! You have done well. Enter here to dwell forever* (39:73), to a place where God has prepared for them things beyond their imaginations. Those who stained the world with bloodshed, sin, and crimes will enter Hell with the shout: *Enter (through) the gates of Hell to dwell therein forever: what an evil abode for the arrogant!* (39:72).

God's being eternally Perfect and infinitely Beautiful requires it. Listen to the birds singing on a spring morning, the murmur of a brook flowing through green fields or deep valleys. Look at the beauty of spectacular green plains and blossoming trees. Watch the sunrise or sunset, the full moon on a cloudless, clear night. All of these and many other sights testify to an amazing, hidden Perfection and unequaled transcendent Beauty, just as sunlight testifies to the sun's existence.

Every manifestation of that hidden Perfection and transcendent, holy Beauty points to the existence of innumerable unseen treasures in each Divine Name. Their Owner desires to see and be "seen." He desires to see His Beauty in two ways: by beholding it in "mirrors of differentiated colors," and via the gaze of dazzled admirers and yearning witnesses.

This is not due to any need, but because of His being eternally Perfect and infinitely Beautiful. Any perfection longs to be known by those who will gaze upon it with admiration and appreciation. Eternal perfection requires eternal manifestation, and the eternal existence of those who will appreciate and admire it. The value of perfection must diminish in its admirer's view if he or she is not eternal. In addition, any non-eternal blessing leaves pain in our hearts when it disappears. If spring did not return next year, we would sigh until we died.

So, true blessing is that which is eternal. But we see in this temporary world that everyone departs after only a brief taste of that Perfection and Beauty—tasting enough to whet but not satiate the appetite, seeing only a faint shadow of the light coming from the Perfection without being fully contented.

Eternal Beauty can never be content with transient admirers. The love of an admirer condemned to permanent separation soon turns to hatred once the thought of separation takes hold. Admiration yields to a bad opinion, and respect yields to contempt. Just as we may be hostile to that which is unknown, we may be opposed to what lies beyond our reach. A finite love will respond to a beauty that deserves infinite admiration with tacit hostility, hatred, and rejection. This is one reason why unbelievers are so hostile to God.

God, the Eternally Beautiful One, shows us only the shadows of His Beauty to arouse in us a desire for its eternal and perfect manifestations. What is more, He will allow us to "see" Him in Paradise in a manner free from any qualitative and quantitative measures or dimensions: *On that day there will be shining faces, gazing upon their Master* (75:22-23).

It follows that we are journeying to a place of eternal joy, a place in which we will receive joy in full measure. In short, just as this world decisively argues the existence of the Majestic Creator, so too do His holy Attributes and Names point to and necessitate the existence of the Hereafter.

God's being the All-Compassionate and Answerer of prayers requires it. God is the Master of infinite compassion and mercy, Who most compassionately fulfills the least need of His lowliest creatures in the most unexpected fashion. He answers the faintest cry of help of His most obscure creature, and responds to all voiced or unvoiced petitions. How could He not heed the greatest petition of His foremost servant and His most beloved creature? How could He not hear and grant such a one's most exalted prayer? The tender solicitude manifested in nurturing weak, young animals shows that the Compassionate Master of the universe exercises His being Master with infinite compassion.

God is also the Answerer of all prayers. Every being prays to God for its needs, by disposition, acts, or words, and God answers these prayers in the most beneficial way. How could God, Who answers the prayer of the least being for its least need, not heed the prayer of humanity's greatest representative, Prophet Muhammad?

Look how he is praying for eternal felicity with such perfect supplication, such sublime worship. It is as if the whole world were praying and supplicating with him, for his worship includes not only that of his followers, but the worship, in its essentials, of all other Prophets, by virtue of their obedience to the same One Master.

He makes his supreme prayer and supplications amid so large a congregation that it is as if all illustrious and perfect ones, from the time of Adam to the present, were following him in prayer and saying "Amen" to his petition. He is petitioning for so universal a need—immortality—that not merely the inhabitants of this Earth, but also those of the heavens and the whole creation, share in his pleas and silently affirm: "Yes, O Master! Accept his prayer; we too desire it." He pleads for everlasting felicity so plaintively that creation is moved to tears and shares in his plea, and with such yearning and longing that if there were not innumerable other reasons and causes for it, a single prayer of that noble being would suffice for the creation of Paradise.

How could the perfect artistry and unequaled beauty of God's being Master, manifested in creation's amazing orderliness, and in the comprehensive mercy thereof, refuse the Prophet's prayer and thereby countenance an extreme ugliness, pitilessness, and discord? How could the All-Sustaining Master hear and grant the smallest and most insignificant desire, but refuse the greatest and most important desire as worthless? Such Beauty could never countenance such ugliness and make itself ugly.

God's being the All-Recording and Preserving requires it. As many things and media conduct sounds and images, so there must be things that record and preserve. This allows us to record and preserve important information. This means that the Ruler is One All-Recording and Preserving, and that whatever takes place, especially that which proceeds from His conscious servants, is of great importance for Him. Thus we can conclude that He must have ordered that all transactions and deeds be recorded and preserved.

The Being Who administers this cosmos never condemns anything to eternal loss or annihilation. He preserves all things in an order and balance that manifest His Knowledge and Wisdom, Will and Power. We see that the substance of every created thing, and all the forms through which it passes, as an individual and as a member of a group, are fashioned in a perfect and pleasing symmetrical orderliness.

Furthermore, the Majestic Preserver preserves many forms of what has perished in human memories, which are like the Supreme Guarded Tablet on which every thing and event were pre-eternally recorded and are preserved, or like an archetypal mirror. The same Majestic Preserver inscribes a compact life history, which is the issue and outcome of that life, in a seed. Thus He causes all things to be preserved in "mirrors" corresponding to outer and inner worlds. Humanity's memories, the tree's fruit, the fruit's kernel, the flower's seed—all manifest the universality and inclusiveness of the law of preservation.

Have you not seen how, for all of spring's flowers and fruits, the records of their deeds, the laws of their formation, and the images of their forms are all inscribed and preserved within a minute seed? The following spring, those records are opened—a form of bringing to account appropriate to them—and another vast world of spring emerges with absolute orderliness and wisdom.

As we mentioned in chapter three, an experiment was conducted to reveal a killer. The suspects were brought to the tree where the crime was committed. The tree showed nothing unusual until the killer was brought under it. Somehow, it had recorded the killer's voice, manner, posture, attitude, or whatever he had displayed during the crime.

All of this shows that God enfolds and preserves everything in such small things as seeds. Human beings are enfolded in sperms and eggs, or in their 46 chromosomes. If they had 44 or 48 chromosomes, they would be completely different beings. Similarly, when they disappear into the ground after death, their most essential part, which has the same meaning for their existence as a seed has for a plant, does not disappear. On the Day of Resurrection, God will rebuild them from that part.

From this comprehensive preserving we can understand what great care the Master of creation devotes to the orderliness of all that occurs under His Rule. He is absolutely attentive to being Sovereign, Sustainer, and Master. Therefore He records, or causes to be recorded, the least event and the smallest service, and preserves the form of all things and events in His Rule in numerous records. This indicates that an important register of deeds will be scrutinized and weighed, and that humanity's record will be opened.

How could we enter an endless sleep in our graves without being questioned about our deeds? How could God's Attribute of Preserving, protecting within absolute orderliness and equilibrium all things in the Heavens and on Earth, allow our acts to remain unsifted and unaccounted for, unweighed in the balance of justice, and not punished or rewarded fittingly? How could an eternal abode not be built according to what we did in the world, and why and how and with what intention we acted therein?

God's being the All-Living and Reviving, and the One Who makes to die, requires it. God revives this vast Earth when it is dead and dry, thereby manifesting His Power by reviving millions of extraordinary species in which He manifests His all-embracing Knowledge in the infinite variations within the complex intermingling of their distinct forms. God turns His servants' attention toward everlasting contentment, assuring them of the Resurrection in His heavenly decrees. He makes the splendor of His being their Master and Nurturer visible. He causes all His creatures to collaborate with each other, turning within the orbit of His Command and Will, to help each other in submission to Him.

The importance He attaches to human beings is shown by His creating them as the most comprehensive and subtle, the most worthy and valued, fruit on the tree of creation, by addressing them without intermediary through revelation and inspiration, and by subjugating all things to them. How could the One Who exercises at every moment His being the All-Reviving condemn anyone to utter annihilation under the soil by not raising him or her to an eternal life? Such an idea is inconceivable.

Indeed, the Almighty Director and Administrator of this world's affairs creates at every moment, on the Earth's finite and transient surface, numerous signs, examples, and indications of the Supreme Gathering and the Plain of Resurrection.

God can destroy and rebuild the world in a different form in which humanity will live eternally. The One Who will bring the next world into being is eminently able to do so. He is absolutely powerful over everything, and the greatest and smallest things are the same in relation to His Power.

He is so powerful that all of creation bears witness to His Power and Majesty. Thus, no one has any reason to doubt that He will raise the dead for the Last Judgment. His Power is such that each He constantly fills and empties the world and renews it every year. He hangs many transient worlds upon the string of time as centuries, years, or even days for a perfect, definite purpose.[37]

He displays the perfection of His Wisdom and the beauty of His art by clothing the Earth in spring, as if it were a single flower. During each spring's gathering, we see how in a few days millions of animal and plant species are assembled and then scattered. All tree and plant roots, and certain animals, are revived and restored exactly as they were. Other animals are re-created in a nearly identical form. Seeds that outwardly appear so alike grow quickly into distinct and differentiated forms, and are brought to full vigor with extraordinary rapidity and facility in absolute orderliness and harmony.

As He can do this, how can we doubt that He will cause the Resurrection to happen and to replace this world with another? The verse: *Your creation and your being raised up are as but the creation and raising up of a single soul* (31:28) announces that the All-Powerful One faces no difficulty in anything, and that creating innumerable individuals is as easy for Him as creating one.

In order to better understand how God can destroy and rebuild the universe, consider the following parables: Let's suppose there was a gifted writer who could copy out in a single hour the confused, half-effaced letters of millions of books on a single sheet without any error or omission, fully and in the best style. If someone told you that she could write from memory a book she had written, one that had fallen into water and become effaced, would you say that she could not, or would you believe that she could?

Or think of a talented ruler who, to demonstrate his power or provide an example, removes mountains with a command, turns his country about, and transforms the sea into dry land. Then imagine a great boulder has rolled down a valley, blocking the path of guests traveling to attend his reception. If someone told you: "The ruler will remove or dissolve the boulder with a command, for he will not leave his guests stranded," would you say that he will not or could not do so?

---

37 There is a constant change and renewal in the universe. Nothing at the present is the same as it the next moment. Modern science accepts this fact. Even some Sufis like Mawlana Jalal al-Din al-Rumi and Muhy al-Din ibn al-'Arabi say that God constantly causes the universe to die and then re-creates it. Since this happens so quickly, it appears that the universe is constant. Modern physics also accepts this.

Or if someone assembled a great army, and you are told that he will summon them to parade in battalion-sized disciplined rows with a trumpet blast after allowing them to rest, would you say" "I don't believe it?"

The All-Glorious, Who from non-being inscribes fresh recruits into His battalions with the command of *Be, and it is,* and ranks with absolute orderliness all living things (even their particles) and thus creates highly disciplined armies—Is it reasonable even to ask how He can make bodies submit to His discipline like obedient soldiers, how He can assemble their mutually related fundamental particles, and all their members composed thereof?

The character of the Divine Power and the way it acts. As the Divine Power comes from the very nature of the Divine Essence, no incapacity can be connected with it. As it is related to the inner, immaterial dimension of existence, no obstacle can interfere with its operation. Also, in its relation to things, Divine Power resembles the Divine laws of nature in that a universal and a particular are the same. We will explain these three arguments below:

First argument. Eternal Power is essential to the Divine Essence. It is an indispensable attribute of Divinity, as the Divine Essence is in one respect identical with Divine Power. No incapacity, which is the opposite of the Infinite, Eternal Power, can occur in Him, for this would mean the existence of opposites within the Infinite Being. Since this is impossible, and impotence cannot occur in the Divine Essence, nothing can interfere with the Divine Power.

In addition, it can contain no degrees, for degrees are manifestations of opposites. Degrees of temperature occur because of the intervention of cold, and degrees of beauty are due to the intervention of ugliness. The same is true of all qualities in the universe. Contingent things and beings contain opposites, for their existence depends not on themselves but on One Who brings them into existence, and because no undiluted quality is essential to their existence. Such degrees and graduations make the world of contingents subject to change and transformation. Since there can be no degrees in the Eternal Divine Power, creating a particle or a galaxy, resurrecting humanity or one human being, or creating spring or a flower are done with exactly the same ease.

Second argument. The Divine Power operates in the inner, spiritual dimension of things (the metaphysical kingdom). The universe is like a two-sided mirror: one side is physical, resembling a mirror's colored face; the other is metaphysical, like the mirror's shining face, and looks to the Creator. The physical side contains all opposites, and so manifests beauty and ugliness, good and evil, and so on. The Majestic Creator of the universe veils the acts of His Power behind observed causes, so that no one should regard His Power's relation to simple things as unbecoming to Him. This is required by His Honor and Majesty. Actually, He has not assigned to causes any real effect upon creation, and this should be so because of His Oneness and Unity.

The metaphysical world is absolutely clear and transparent, and the grossness of the physical world is not involved with it. The Divine Power is directly operative in this realm, where "cause and effect" has no effect. Obstacles cannot interfere, and creating a particle is equivalent to forming the sun.

To conclude, the Divine Power is simple and infinite, an indispensable Attribute of the Divine Essence. The realm in which it operates directly is clear, refined, and transparent, and nothing opposes or intervenes in it. Thus in the realm of Power, there is no difference between a community and an individual, a particular and a universal, and so on, for everything is the same.

Third argument. The Divine Power operates like a law having the same relationship with every thing, regardless of size or quantity. Consider the following connections. Transparency, reciprocity, balance, orderliness, abstraction, and obedience are the phenomena in the universe which render the many equal to the few, and the great equal to the small.

- *First connection: Transparency.* The same sun is reflected on the ocean's surface and in a drop of water. If the Earth were made up of pieces of glass, the sun would be reflected in each piece without hindrance and without one interfering with the other. If the sun were a conscious, independent being with the willpower to reflect its own light, it would not be more difficult for it to give light to, or be reflected in, a single particle than the whole Earth.

- *Second connection: Reciprocity.* Imagine that someone holding a lighted candle is standing in the center of a large circle of people, each of whom is holding a mirror. The resulting reflections would be the same in each mirror, and no reflection would hinder another.

- *Third connection: Balance.* Suppose that we were weighing a pair of things, such as two suns, with a balance of very precise measurement. Any extra force exerted upon either scale, no matter how slight, would disturb the balance.

- *Fourth connection: Orderliness.* A large ship can be steered as easily as a small toy, for it has an orderly system and all of its parts are interrelated.

- *Fifth connection: Abstraction.* A living creature's size has no bearing upon its real essence or nature. Any species' essence or nature, because it is abstract and incorporeal, is the same for all members irrespective of size. Differences in individualized forms do not cause any confusion. A minnow has the same essence or nature as a basking-shark, since both are fish. A micro-organism has the same essence as a rhinoceros, since both are living animals.

- *Sixth connection: Obedience.* A commander moves an army as easily as a soldier by ordering: "March!" The reality of obedience in the universe is as follows: Everything in the universe inclines toward its own perfection. This inclination grows into a need, an increased need becomes a yearning, and an increased yearning becomes an attraction. Inclination, need, yearning, and attraction all work as Divine laws, and all operate in things to realize their perfection. Their relative perfection is the relative existence that gives effect to all their potentialities. This is why the universe's obedience to the Divine Command *"Be!"* is the same as a particle's obedience. All creation obeys this order, which comes from the Creator's Eternal Will, via the same forces of inclination, need, yearning, and attraction, all of which are urged to operate on all creatures by the same Divine Will. The power of this obedience is best displayed by water, which cracks iron or even breaks it into pieces, when it receives the order to freeze.

Seeing that contingent forces, all of which are defective, limited, weak, and devoid of creativity, display such effects, we can see that everything is equally susceptible to the Divine Power's order. This Power is infinite, eternal, absolutely perfect, and can bring the universe into existence from non-existence. It also can manifest itself through its grand works, which fascinate and astound all conscious beings. Nothing is difficult for it. The six above-mentioned connections do not pass any judgment upon the Divine Power, which would be impossible for created beings. Rather, they enable us to have some grasp of the matter.

To summarize this argument: The Divine Power is infinite and an indispensable Attribute of the Supreme Being. It operates directly upon the metaphysical dimension of things, which is free of all obstacles and differences. This domain is in direct contact with the Divine Power. With respect to creation, it is equally possible for all things to come into material existence or not. Also, it strictly obeys the Divine laws of creation. We can conclude that it is equally easy for the Divine Power to create something large or small. Thus, it is as easy for this Power to quicken all creation on the Last Day as to revive an insect in spring. Given this, the Divine announcement of *Your creation and your being raised up are as but as a single soul* (31:28), is true and accurate. This proves that the Agent Who will destroy and re-create the universe on the Last Day can do so.

All Prophets, saints, and religious scholars agree on the Resurrection and the afterlife. The report of two specialists in a given area gives people contentment and assurance, and is preferable to the many opposing views of non-specialists. Throughout history, more than 100,000 Prophets and countless saints, religious scholars, philosophers, and scientists have believed and reported that this world is temporary, subject to perishing, and that it will be succeeded by a new, eternal life where people will be called to account and judged accordingly.

Moreover, even if one reliable reporter warned that a particular way carried a 1 percent risk of the traveler perishing on it, that way would lose its attraction because of the resulting distress and fear. However, countless truthful, authoritative reporters (Prophets, saints, and pure, verifying scholars), and with demonstrable proofs of their truth, have warned that misguidance and dissipation carry a 100 percent risk of the gallows of death and punishment.

By contrast, belief and worship remove such gallows and imprisonment, and change the grave into a door opening onto an eternal treasury, a palace of lasting happiness. Is it reasonable to reject this report and heed this warning? Why should we seek to contradict so many reliable persons, who were never heard to lie, who have been acknowledged as the most truthful of humanity, and accuse billions of people who have followed them of following liars and fallacies?

In conclusion, the consensus of the Prophets, the elect and most truthful of humanity, and saints and verifying religious scholars on the Resurrection and afterlife is an irrefutable proof.

QUR'ANIC ARGUMENTS

Scientific findings like the second law of thermodynamics show that existence is on the way to destruction. For example, the universe could be destroyed by the collision of two planets. Existence, with all its divisions, is an extremely delicately calculated "organism," a system whose parts are subtly interdependent. A human body is made up of about trillions of cells. As one deformed, cancerous cell may kill the whole body, any serious deformation in the universe may lead to its death. Sometimes death comes unexpectedly and without any visible, diagnosed reason. So, could the universe die suddenly, unexpectedly, without a visible reason, or because of a "disease" like a "heart attack"? Could our world be suffering from the terminal phase of cancer because of our misuse of it?

God's universal acts point to the Resurrection. The Qur'an argues for the Resurrection. To impress upon the human heart the wonder of what the Almighty will accomplish in the Hereafter, and to prepare the human mind to accept and understand it, the Qur'an presents the wonder of what He accomplishes here to prepare us for it. It gives examples of God's comprehensive acts in the macro-cosmos and, at times, presents His overall disposal of the macro-, normo-, and micro-cosmoses (the universe, humanity, and atoms, respectively).

For example, the following Qur'anic verse stresses God's Power and, by mentioning various facts, calls us to have conviction in our meeting with Him in the Hereafter:

> God is He Who raised the heavens without any pillars that you can see, then He established Himself upon the Throne (of authority; having shaped the universe and made it dependent upon certain laws, He exercises His absolute authority over it), and subjected the sun and the moon (to His command); each runs (its course) for an appointed term. He regulates all affairs, expounding the signs, that you may believe with certainty in the meeting with your Master. (13:2)

The first origination of the universe and humanity indicate their "second origination." The Qur'an presents the phenomenon of the universe's creation, which it defines as the first origination (56:62), while describing the raising of the dead as the second origination (53:47), to prove the Resurrection. It also directs our attention to our own origin, arguing:

> You see how you progressed—from a drop of sperm to a drop of blood, to a blood clot suspended on the wall of the womb, from a suspended blood clot to a formless lump of flesh, and from a formless lump of flesh to human form—how, then, can you deny your second creation? It is just the same as the first, or even easier [for God to accomplish]. (22:5; 23:13-16)

The Qur'an makes analogies between the Resurrection and His deeds in this world. It sometimes alludes to the deeds God will perform in the future and in the Hereafter in such a way that we are convinced of them by drawing analogies to what we observe here. It also shows similar events here and makes comparisons between them and the Resurrection. One example is as follows:

> Has not man seen that We have created him from a sperm-drop? Then lo, he is a manifest adversary. And he has coined for Us a similitude, and has forgotten the fact of his creation, saying: "Who will revive these bones when they have rotted away?" Say: "He will revive them Who produced them at the first, for He is Knower of all creation."[38] Who has made for you fire from the green tree, and behold! you kindle from it. Is not He Who created the heavens and the Earth able to create the like of them. Aye, that He is! For He is the All-Wise Creator. (36:78-81)

The Qur'an also likens the Resurrection to the Earth's springtime rejuvenation or revival following its death in winter. It mentions how God disposes of atoms and molecules while creating human beings in stages. Nature dies in winter but is revived during spring, when dry pieces of wood come into leaf, blossom, and yield fruit. All of these are similar (but not identical) to the ones that came into being the previous year. Innumerable plant seeds that fell into the ground during the previous autumn germinate under and grow into different plants without the least confusion. The raising of the dead on the Day of Judgment will be like this:

> Among His signs is that you see the earth dry and barren; and when We send down rain on it, it stirs to life and swells. Surely God Who gives the dead earth life will raise the dead also to life. Indeed, He has power over all things. (41:39)

> O mankind! If you are in doubt concerning the Resurrection, (consider that) We created you of dust, then of semen, then of a fertilized ovum suspended on the wall of the womb, then of a lump of flesh shaped and unshaped, so that We demonstrate to you Our power. And We keep in the wombs what We please to an appointed term, and afterwards We bring you forth as infants, then We cause you to grow up, that you reach your prime. Among you some die (young) and some are sent back to the feeblest phase of age so that they know nothing after they had knowledge. You sometimes see the Earth dry and barren. But when We pour down rain on it, it trembles, and swells, and grows

---

38 That is, you see that trees come to life again and grow green. Your bones resemble dry branches, yet you refuse to recognize the likeness in the re-animation of those bones and regard their re-animation as utterly improbable.

of every pleasant pair. That is so because God is the Truth, and He it
is Who gives life to the dead, and He is powerful over all things. (22:5-
6)

Does man think that he will be left to himself uncontrolled (without
purpose)? Was he not a drop of fluid which gushed forth? Then he
became a clinging clot; then He shaped and fashioned, and made of
him a pair, the male and female. Is He then not able to raise the dead
to life? (75:36-40)

Look at the imprints of God's Mercy: how He gives life to the Earth
after its death. Lo! He verily is the Reviver of the dead (in the same
way), and He is able to do all things. (30:50)

God has brought you forth from earth like a plant. And to earth
He will restore you. Then He will bring you back fresh. (71:17-18)

In *sura*s 81, 82, and 84, the All-Mighty alludes to the Resurrection and the
vast revolutions and Masterly deeds that shall take place at that time. He uses
images that we can relate, by analogy, to what we see here—scenes witnessed
in autumn or spring—and then, with awe in our hearts, accept what the intellect
might otherwise refuse. As giving even the general meaning of these three
*sura*s would take a great deal of time, let's take one verse: *When the pages are
spread out* (81:10). This implies that during the Resurrection, everyone's deeds
will be revealed on a written page.

At first, this strikes one as strange and incomprehensible. But as the *sura*
indicates, just as the renewal of spring parallels another resurrection, "spreading
out the pages" has a very clear parallel. Every fruit-bearing tree and flowering
plant has its own properties, functions, and deeds. It worships according to its
glorification of God, which is how it manifests His Names. Its deeds and life
record are inscribed in each seed that will emerge next spring. With the tongue
of shape and form, these new trees or flowers offer an eloquent exposition of
the life and deeds of the original tree or flower. Through their various parts, they
spread out the page of its deeds. He Who says: *When the pages are spread out*
is the same Being Who achieves these feats in a very wise, prudent, efficient,
and subtle way, as dictated by His Names All-Wise, All-Preserving, All-
Sustaining and Training, and All-Subtle.

Other issues of the Resurrection can be dealt with similarly. However to
help reach the truth, I will add the following:

The verse *When the sun is folded up*, in addition to referring to a brilliant image by the verb "fold up," alludes to its parallel in this world:

- *First:* The All-Mighty drew aside the veils of non-being, then of ether and the heavens, to bring forth from His treasury of Mercy and show to the world a jewel-like lamp (the sun) to lighten that world. After closing the world, He will rewrap that jewel and remove it.

- *Second:* The sun may be considered an official charged with diffusing light and alternately winding light and darkness around the Earth's head. Every evening it is ordered to gather up this light and be concealed. It sometimes is prevented from carrying out this task completely, due to the presence of clouds or the moon.

Just as that official regularly has its goods and ledgers gathered up in this world, so one day it will be relieved of its duties. Even if there were no reason for the sun's dismissal, the two spots on its face (now small and liable to grow) may grow to the point that it will take back, by its Master's command, the light that it wraps around the Earth's head.

And, God will wrap that light around its own head, saying: "Come, you have no more duty toward the Earth. Go to Hell and burn there all who worshipped you and thus insulted such an obedient servant by ascribing faithlessness to your Creator." With its dark, scarred face, the sun announces the decree: *When the sun is folded up.*

The universe is like a book unfolded, and its destruction will be like rolling it up again. At the end of time, the universe's destruction will be as easy for God as rolling up a scroll. As He unrolled it at the beginning, He will roll it up and, through the manifestation of His absolute Power, re-create it in a much better and different form:

> On that day We shall roll up the heavens like a scroll rolled up for books. As We originated the first creation, so We shall bring it forth again. It is a promise (binding) upon Us. We shall fulfill it (as We promised it). (21:104)

Bringing the dead to life is not more difficult for God than creating the universe. Many Qur'anic verses draw our attention to God's Power, for which creating a flower is as easy as creating the spring or the world:

> Have they not seen that God, Who created the heavens and the earth and was not wearied by their creation, is able to give life to the dead? He has power over everything. (46:33)

In many verses, the Qur'an means: "The One Who will resurrect you is the One before Whom the whole creation is like His obedient soldier: It bows its head submissively whenever it hears the command *'Be!' and it is.*"

Again, by such similar verses as *Glory be to Him in Whose hand is the dominion over all things*, the Qur'an affirms that He controls everything and has the key to everything. He turns over night and day, winter and summer, as easily as if He were turning a page in a book. He is All-Powerful and Majestic. He closes the world and opens the Hereafter.

Two mighty "streams" flow in creation opposite to each other. As pointed out earlier, the universe contains two opposed and clashing elements that have spread everywhere and become rooted. The result is pairs of opposites: good and evil, benefit and harm, perfection and defect, light and darkness, guidance and misguidance, belief and unbelief, obedience and rebellion, and fear and love.

These opposed elements eventually will lead to eternity in two different directions, and be materialized as Paradise and Hell. The eternal world will be made up of this transitory world's essential elements, which will be given permanence. Paradise and Hell are, in fact, the two opposite fruits growing on the tree of creation's two branches, the two results of the chain of creation, the two cisterns being filled by the two streams of things and events, and the two poles to which beings are flowing in waves.

As declared in: *Keep apart on this day, O you sinners* (36:59), God will separate the good from the wicked in the Hereafter, and treat each group according to how it lived in this world. This is simply what His absolute Justice requires.

The Qur'an warns humanity of its responsibility in return for God's blessings. Many Qur'anic verses mention God's bounties or blessings to humanity, and warn us that we will have to account for our gratitude or ingratitude. In other words: "O humanity! Will the One Who bestowed His bounty upon you leave you free to behave as you wish, and then enter into the grave to sleep permanently without rising again?"

CHAPTER 6
BELIEF IN THE RESURRECTION AND
THE AFTERLIFE IS UNIVERSAL

BELIEF IN THE RESURRECTION AND
THE AFTERLIFE IS UNIVERSAL

Eschatology is the branch of systematic theology that deals with the doctrines of the last things (*ta eschata*). Although the Greek title is a comparatively recent introduction, it has largely supplanted its Latin equivalent *De Novissimis* in modern usage.

As a first step, a distinction may be made between the eschatology of the individual and that of the race and the universe at large. The former, setting out from the doctrine of personal immortality, or at least of survival in some form after death, seeks to ascertain the soul's temporary or eternal fate or condition, and how much this life affects the future life. The latter deals with events like the Resurrection and final judgment, and with the signs and portents preceding and accompanying those events. Both aspects belong to the usual concept of eschatology.

BELIEF IN THE AFTERLIFE IN NON-ISLAMIC SOCIETIES

The universality of religious beliefs, including some kind of existence after death, is generally admitted by modern anthropologists. Some exceptions have been claimed to exist; but on closer scrutiny the provided evidence breaks down in so many cases that we can say that there are no exceptions. Among ancient peoples, the truth and purity of eschatological beliefs vary with the purity of the idea of God and prevailing moral standards. Some early peoples seem to limit existence after death to the good (with extinction for the wicked), as the Nicaraguas, or to men of rank, as the Tongas; while the various peoples of Greenland, New Guinea, and others seem to hold the possibility of a second death in the other world or on the way to it.

Let's look at some of these beliefs more closely.

Aztec. A person's social position and circumstances of death were determining factors for his or her destiny in the next existence. We do not hear of any retribution after death based on one's conduct during this life. This might have been expected, since the confession of sins and penance (e.g., asceticism or temple service) were common. Perhaps they were important only for happiness and success in this world.

The dead were distributed among several death realms. Mictlan was intended for the majority. Situated in the north, it belonged to the lower regions and was ruled by Mictlantecuhtli, a frightening skeletal figure surrounded by bats, spiders, owls, and his consort Mictecacihuatl. The journey to his kingdom led through nine subterranean worlds and took 4 years. As in other Indian tales of journeys to the land of the dead, especially among North American Indians, numerous obstacles were encountered: a difficult river, mountains, icy winds, and fierce beasts. Amulets buried with the dead offered protection.

Other death realms were lighter in tone. Those who drowned, were struck by lightning, or died from leprosy came to Tlaloc's paradise (Tlalocan) in the south. Here, they enjoyed a pleasant existence with abundant fruit, corn, and beans. According to Sahagun, sorrow was unknown. Tlalocan has a long history in the Mesoamerican conceptual world. There is an exceedingly beautiful temple painting from Teotihuacan, in the early classical period, depicting its delights: a fortunate land with its lake, rivers, and cacao trees as the abode of many dancing, singing, and swimming people, all full of life and motion.

Another paradise was "the house of the sun," the sun god's kingdom in the east. Its inhabitants were warriors killed in battle and prisoners sacrificed to the gods. The sun summoned them and invited them to share his joy. They enjoyed the fragrance of marvelous flowers and feigned combat. When the sun rose in the east, they greeted him by beating their shields with loud shouts of joy.

The sun also had a propitious land in the west, "the corn house," for women who died in childbirth. In the afternoon they escorted the sun on its way. At night they sometimes returned to the Earth, and their ghostly apparitions frightened women and small children.[39]

Maya. Landa writes that the Mayans had a paradise with its delights, including abundant food and drink in the holy tree's shadow. They also had Mitnal, a subterranean hell for the wicked and evil, where hunger, cold, and sorrow tormented them. The "death god" Hunhau presided over this gloomy world. Little is known about the ruler of the paradise.[40]

Inca. If sinners did not make a full confession, they would be stricken with the wrath of the powers in this life, and after death would starve and freeze in a place deep in the Earth's interior, where their only food would be stories. Those who led virtuous lives and confessed their sins would lead a happy existence with abundant food and drink in the sun god's heaven. Members of the

39 Ake Hultkrantz, *The Religion of the American Indians*, The University of California Press, Los Angeles: 1979.
40 ibid.

aristocracy, intended for a higher world, ended up there regardless of how they lived.

Now, coming to the more advanced societies, we shall glance briefly at the eschatologies of Babylonia and Assyria, Egypt, India, Persia, Greece, and of Judaism and Christianity.

Babylonia and Assyria. In the ancient Babylonian religion, with which the Assyrian is substantially identical, retribution seems to be mostly confined to the present life. Virtue is rewarded by the Divine bestowal of strength, prosperity, long life, numerous offspring, and the like. Wickedness is punished by temporal calamities.

As for the afterlife, it was believed that a kind of semi-material ghost, shade, or double (*ekimmu*) survived physical death. When the body was buried (or, less commonly, cremated), the ghost descended to the underworld to join the departed. In the *Day of Ishtar*, the underworld to which she descended to look for her deceased lover and the "waters of life" is described in gloomy colors, a feature found in the other descriptions. It is the "pit," the "land of no return," the "house of darkness," the "place where dust is their bread, and their food is mud." It is infested with demons, who, at least in Ishtar's case, can inflict various chastisements for sins committed in the upper world.

This ancient religion suggests a brighter hope in the form of a resurrection, which some infer from the belief in the "waters of life" and from references to Marduk (or Merodach) as "one who brings the dead to life."

Egypt. Ancient Egyptian religion has a highly developed and comparatively elevated eschatology. Leaving aside some conflicting elements, we will refer to what is most prominent in its eschatology taken at its highest and best.

Pious Egyptians looked forward to a full, unending life with the sun god Osiris (who journeys daily through the underworld), and identification with him and the subsequent right to be called by his name, as the ultimate goal after death. The departed are habitually called the "living," the coffin is the "chest of the living," and the tomb is the "lord of life."

It is not merely the disembodied spirit that continues to live, but the soul with certain bodily organs and functions suited to the new life's conditions. In the elaborate anthropology underlying Egyptian eschatology, several constituents of the individual are distinguished. The most important is the *ka*, a kind of semi-material double. Those who pass the judgment after death have the use of these several constituents, separated by death, restored.

Egyptians believed that every person was composed of three essential elements: body, *ba,* and *ka.*

- The body is the physical body and is unique to each individual. As a person gets older, it ages and changes. The Egyptians' expressed the idea of growing up as a process of "making changes," with death being the last change.
- Each person has a unique, non-physical *ba. Ba* is sometimes translated as "manifestation," and can be thought of as the sum total of all non-physical things that make a person unique. In this sense, *ba* is very similar to personality or character. In the afterlife, it is represented as a bird, often with a human head.
- Each person has a *ka* (life-force), which is the difference between being alive and being dead. The *ka* is common to all living people and the gods. In the beginning, the creator made the ka, which enters each person's body at birth. The *ka* is not a physical entity, although it has a definite physical connection. In the plural, *ka* means "sustenance," linking it to the idea of food. In fact, ancient Egyptians brought food to a tomb as an offering to the deceased's *ka.* But since the ka is not strictly physical, the food was to be eaten by the deceased or the deceased's *ka,* and its life-preserving force was offered to the *ka.*

At death, the *ba* and *ka* were separated from the body but did not die. In the New Kingdom (post-1570 bce) period and after, this separation was effected through the Opening of the Mouth ritual, in which the *ba* and *ka* were released to go to the next world.

In the next world, or the underworld, the goal was to live with one's *ka.* For this to happen, the ka had to be summoned back to the body and recognize it. But since the body by then had been mummified, it had to rely on its *ba* to seek out its *ka.* During the night, when the sun god Ra was said to visit the underworld, the *ba* could roam freely in the underworld or to popular places in this world. Its anchor in this world was the body. When Ra left the underworld, the *ba* had to return to this world, because together they are part of the same whole being.

The *ba* also had to overcome many potential dangers in the underworld. If it succeeded, it would reunite with the *ka* and form the *akh.* Egyptians believed that there were only three kinds of beings in the hereafter: the dead, the gods, and the *akh*s (those who have transitioned to the new life in the next world, where they live with the gods). The dead are those who failed to make the transition. Thus they were held to have "died again," without hope of renewed life.

Egyptians believed that death was the end of physical life. But, it also was through death that one could be renewed and live an eternal life free of such physical limitations as age or poverty, just as the once-mortal god Osiris had. One's renewal did not come about here, though, but in "Nun," the mysterious underworld of primeval waters that was separate from this world. One could not see it or get to it by normal means; the only ways were through imagination and knowledge of the sun's path.

Paintings on tomb walls and coffins usually depict this other underworld a strange and mysterious place. In fact, the dead often were called "those whose place is hidden or mysterious." As mummies, they were said to sink into this endless, dark, and chaotic place. The underworld was held to be separated from the real world by a wide stream, and to have a great river flowing through it. This land had water, plants, and trees, where the dead, once they achieved resurrection, would grow crops to live on. This region of the underworld sometimes was called the Ealu fields.

According to the book of *Amduat,* the underworld was divided into twelve departments (or hours), and twelve portals representing the 12 hours of night between sunset and sunrise. But the underworld's time differed from that of the Earth's, for each hour in the former represented an entire lifetime in the latter.

The sun god Ra travels in his boat on the great river, bringing order and life to each department in turn. Along the way his boat may come across the sandbank of Apophis. This monster of chaos has the shape of a giant serpent and, being Ra's enemy, tries to wreck his boat.

The most important of the obstacles that could stand in the way of the *ba*'s reunion with the *ka*, and the deceased's resurrection, was the judgment of the dead. We know of this mostly from one of the latest and most popular collections of spells, the *Book of the Dead,* which became the standard for funerary literature from the 18th Dynasty (the New Kingdom) until the end of ancient Egyptian civilization. A great deal of relevant information is contained in "Spell 125."

The deceased would begin to recite a formula called the Negative Confession, part of which follows:

> I have not done falsehood against people. I have not impoverished my associates. I have done no wrong in the Place of Truth. I have not learned that which is not. I have done no evil. I have not

made people labor daily in excess of what was due to be done for me.

These statements corresponded with the desire to separate one from his or her sins, the ultimate goal of the judgment. As this confession was recited, the balance's scales would either stay in equilibrium, indicating that one's heart was not heavy (the truth was being told), or else tip, indicating that one's heart was heavy with falsehood. Anubis would verify the results, bring the scales in balance, and reassure the confessor.[41] Thoth, god of the written word, would record the results.

Additionally, the one being judged also would have spoken to his or her heart from "Spell 30b":

> O my heart that I had from my mother! O my heart that I had from my mother! O my heart of my different ages! Do not stand up as a witness against me. Do not be opposed to me in the tribunal. Do not be hostile to me in the presence of the Keeper of the Balance …"

Assuming that all went well, as it usually did if one made it to the Hall of Two Truths, a general verdict would be given in which the truthfulness of the judged would be validated. After this, the person could receive offerings and take bread with Osiris, confirming his or her transfer to the order of the afterlife. The person also would receive a parcel of land on which to live eternally.

The principle value in achieving this eternal extension of one's life is the promise it holds in fulfilling one's life begun on Earth. Those who were debilitated in life by crippling diseases, who suffered from poverty, or who were barren would be given an opportunity to fulfill their desires in a new place without obstacles. The dream of an ideal life held on Earth could now be realized.

India. In the Vedas, the earliest historical form of Indian religion, eschatological belief is simpler and purer than in the Brahministic and Buddhist forms that succeeded it. Individual immortality is clearly taught. There is a kingdom of the dead, with distinct realms for the good and the wicked, ruled by Yama. The good dwell in a realm of light and share in the gods' feasts; the wicked are banished to a place of "nethermost darkness." Already in the later Vedas, however, retribution begins to be ruled more by ceremonial observances than by

---

41 Anubis, the Egyptian god who presided over mummification, was presumed to have much knowledge about the dead.

strictly moral tests. On the other hand, there is no trace as yet of the dreary doctrine of transmigration, although critics profess to discover the germs of later pantheism.

In Brahminism, retribution gains in prominence and severity. However, it becomes hopelessly involved in transmigration, and is made more dependent either on sacrificial observances or theosophical knowledge. Though there are numerous heavens and hells for the reward and punishment of every degree of merit and demerit, these are only preludes to further rebirths in higher or lower forms. Pantheistic absorption in Brahma, the world-soul and only reality, with the consequent extinction of individual personality, is the only solution to the "problem" of existence, the only salvation to which a person may look forward. But this salvation is for the few, namely, those who have acquired a perfect knowledge of Brahma. Most people, who cannot rise to this high philosophic wisdom, may gain a temporary heaven via sacrificial observances, but they are destined to undergo further births and deaths.

Buddhism. Buddhism (Sanskrit: "enlightened one") was founded in India by Siddharta Gautama Buddha (ca. 563-ca. 483 bce) Under the Bodhi tree (the tree of enlightenment), Prince Gautama became aware of the four basic truths: Human existence is pain, the cause of pain is desire, pain ceases via emancipation from desire, and the cessation of pain may be attained via the eightfold way of deliverance.

This way involves right knowledge of these four truths, right intention, right speech, right action, right occupation, right effort, right control of sensations and ideas, and right concentration. This way promises to end suffering (which feeds on desire) and lead to Nirvana (Sanskrit: "being extinguished") or a complete state of peace. The Buddhist scriptures exist in Pali (Sri Lanka) and Sanskrit (India).

Two basic doctrines are karma (Sanskrit: "action, faith"), the belief that old deeds are rewarded or punished in this or subsequent lives, and rebirth or the transmigration of souls. Mahayana Buddhism, which arose around the time of Christ, teaches that individuals can attain Nirvana and also can become Buddhas in order to save others.

Buddhism, which includes the worship of gods and various syncretistic features, has two forms: Hinayana (Sanskrit: little vehicle) or Theravada (Pali: old doctrine) Buddhism (found in Burma, Sri Lanka, Thailand, and elsewhere), and Mahayana (Sanskrit: great vehicle) Buddhism (found in China, Japan, Korea, Mongolia, Tibet, and elsewhere). Mahayana Buddhists believe that the right path of a follower will lead to the redemption of humanity. Hinayana Buddhists believe that each person is responsible for his or her own fate.

Along with these doctrines, there are other Buddhist beliefs like Zen Buddhism (Japan) and the Hindu Tantric Buddhism (Tibet). Zen Buddhism is a mixture of Buddhism as it arrived from India and original Japanese beliefs. Hindu Tantric Buddhism is a mixture of Indian Buddhism and original pre-Buddhist Tibetan beliefs such as magic, ghosts and tantras (highly mystical and symbolic practices).

Buddhism is usually regarded as a religion without a god or eschatology. This must be largely due to the fact that it dwells on the individual's spiritual perfection and purification and a harmonious social life. The Buddha stressed the supremacy of ethics, and his outlook was definitely practical and empirical. In fact, he did not tolerate any doctrines that appeared to divert the mind from the central problem of suffering, the cause of suffering and its removal, and the urgency of the moral task. Therefore it cannot be said that Buddhism directly and absolutely rejects belief in a Supreme Being.

Wendy Erickson, a Canadian writer who became an agnostic while an atheist after studying God and Revelation, drew on the "objective" nature of God to make a significant point here:

> In his book, *Medusa's Hair*, Gananath Obeyesekeri has shown us that even today Buddhist ascetics in India mystically experience the divine as a painful (and simultaneously ecstatic) possession by another being that completely takes over their bodies.
>
> Experience has led people in all religious traditions to make very different faith statements about the "objective" nature of God or Ultimate Reality. Buddhists experience the Ultimate as Oneness, Creativity, or Consciousness. Jews, Christians and Muslims have sensed the Ultimate as transcendent Love, Power, and, yes, creativity too. Monistic Hindus perceive the Ultimate as a hidden Self, or Atman, which is one with the Godhead, Brahman. When Love is the predominant sense, transcendence is often sought after through worship and compassion toward others. Believers seek to get beyond themselves by recognizing that the world does not revolve around them; there is an Ultimate Reality that exists beyond their selves, is much bigger than them and, in some sense, more real. Prayer can be seen as one way for a believer to cultivate a sense of being in God's presence. This Reality (God) also exists within each individual.[42]

---

42 See http://atheism.about.com.

What Buddha said about his faith and mission demonstrates that, rather than rejecting a faith or a transcendent reality, his real aim was to found a society on moral values and the cessation of pain in individuals:

> Bear always in mind what it is that I have not elucidated, and what it is that I have elucidated. And what have I not elucidated? I have not elucidated that the world is eternal; I have not elucidated that the world is not eternal; ... I have not elucidated that the soul and the body are identical; I have not elucidated that the monk who has attained (the *arahat*) exists after death; I have not elucidated that the *arahat* does not exist after death; ... I have not elucidated that the *arahat* neither exists nor does not exist after death. And why have I not elucidated this? Because this profits not, nor has to do with the fundamentals of religion; therefore I have not elucidated this. And what have I elucidated? Misery have I elucidated; the origin of misery have I elucidated; the cessation of misery have I elucidated; and the path leading to the cessation of misery have I elucidated. And why have I elucidated this? Because this does profit, has to do with the fundamentals of religion, and tends to absence of passion, to knowledge, supreme wisdom, and Nirvana.[43]

In Buddhism, meditating on impermanence is a traditional antidote to craving and attachment. You can hope to control and possess only that which is unchanging. Like a stream of flickering phenomena, life is ultimately ungraspable. So you begin to see that craving, trying to hold onto things to gain security from them, is doomed to fail from the start—there is nothing to hold onto. Ultimately things are like water, flowing through your fingers as you try to grasp them.

Life does not begin at birth or end at death; rather, it is a link in an infinite series of lives, each of which is conditioned and determined by acts done in previous lives. Relief from rebirth, which results in eternal life, is the goal, as indicated by such terms as *moksa* (deliverance) and Nirvana. Nirvana is the end of the cycles of birth, death, and re-birth; the end of pain; and union with the Ultimate reality, and therefore gaining eternity. Thus, Nirvana can be viewed as the "paradise" of the individual.

Hinduism. Dr. Arnold J. Toynbee points out in *A Study of History* that the principal civilizations placed different degrees of emphasis on specific lines of

---

43 Henry Clarke Warren, *Buddhism in Translation*, Harvard University Press: 1922, p. 122; John B. Noss, *Man's Religions*, "Majjhima Nikaya," Macmillan, New York: 1956, p.166.

activity. Greek civilization, for instance, displays a manifest tendency toward a prominently aesthetic outlook on life as a whole. Indian civilization, on the other hand, shows an equally manifest tendency toward a predominantly religious outlook. Toynbee's remark sums up what has been observed by many other scholars. Indeed, the study of Hinduism has to be, in large measure, a study of the general Hindu outlook on life.

With respect to life, death, and life after death, the inseparable unity of the material and spiritual worlds forms the foundation of Indian culture and determines the whole character of Indian social ideals. Every individual life, whether mineral, vegetable, animal, or human, has a beginning and an end. This creation and destruction, appearance and disappearance, are of the essence of the world process and equally originate in the past, present, and future. According to this view, then, every individual ego or separate expression of the general will to life must be regarded as having reached a certain stage of its own cycle.

The Upanisads, the most famous and widely accepted Hindu texts, recognize intuition rather than reason as a path to ultimate truth. They are supposed to be 108 or more in number. Twelve are generally recognized as the principal units. The *Isa Upanisad* begins with the statement that whatever exists in this world is enveloped by the Supreme. The soul is saved by renunciation and the absence of possessiveness.

The *Mundaka Upanisad* contains the verse that is the germ of the *Bhagavad Gita*. People who act and are attached to the world are pursuing a futile path, and this Upanisad accordingly declares:

> Let the wise person, having examined the world and perceived the motives and the results of actions, realize that as from a blazing fire sparks proceed, living souls originate from the indestructible Brahman and return to Him. All doubts disappear, and the attachment to work subsides when the Supreme Being is cognized.

The *Bhagavad Gita*, a main source of Hindu belief and philosophy, contains the essence of Hindu teaching about the duties of life as well as of spiritual obligations. Everyone has his or her allotted duties. Sin arises not from the nature of the work itself, but from the disposition with which the work is performed. When it is performed without attachment to the result, it cannot tarnish the soul and impede its quest.

True Yoga consists of acquiring experience and passing through life in harmony with the ultimate laws of equanimity, non-attachment to the fruits of action, and faith in the Supreme Spirit's pervasiveness. As absorption in that Spirit can be attained along several paths, no path is to be exclusively preferred or disdained. These doctrines have been interpreted as marking a Protestant movement stressing the personality of God and His accessibility to devotion. While following the Hindu ideal of the Asramas, the *Bhagavad Gita* emphasizes the importance of knowledge, charity, penance, and worship, and does not decry life as evil.

Later on, the fully organized Bhakti movement leading to Vaisnavism and Saivism arose. The ancient Vaisnava mystics and saints in the south were known as Alvars, and the Vaisnava teachers as Acaryas. They had a powerful exponent of these views in Ramanuja (d. 1137?), who attacked the Advaita interpretation of the *Upanisads* and recognized three ultimate realities: God, Soul, and Matter (the last two being dependent on the first).

The next important milestone is the advent of Sankara (d. 820). In his short but marvelously active life, he traveled throughout the country, refuted atheistic and materialistic systems of thought, and wrote commentaries on the *Upanisads,* the *Brahma Sutra,* and the *Bhagavad Gita.* He interpreted these scriptures and built up his thesis with wonderful clarity and depth of exposition. He remolded Indian thought and destroyed many dogmas. His great capacity for deep feeling and emotional expression was combined with a relentless logic.

Sankara's contribution to philosophy is his blending of the doctrines of karma and *maya,* which culminated in a logical exposition of the idea of non-dualism: The entire universe consisting of *namarupa* (names and forms) is only an illusion; Brahman, infinite consciousness, is the sole reality. The objects of Sankara's quest were its attainment and the annihilation of the great illusion of the universe (*maya*) by a process of realization.

One of the most influential and intrinsically valuable religious writings in India is *Saiva Siddhanta.* It recognizes three entities: God, the Soul or the aggregate of souls, and bondage. Bondage denotes the aggregate of elements that fetter the soul and hold it back from union with God. In one of its aspects it is malam, the taint clinging to the soul. In another aspect it is *maya,* the material cause of the world.

The peculiarity of the *Saiva Siddhanta* doctrine, which calls itself Suddhadvaita, is its difference from Vedanta Monism. God pervades and energizes all souls and, nevertheless, stands apart. This concept of the absolute is clear from the Tamil word for God, *Kadavul,* meaning that which transcends (*kada*) all things and is yet the heart (*ul*) of all things. When the absolute becomes manifest, it is as force (*sakti*), of which the universe is the product.

After many centuries, during which Hindu religion and philosophy underwent certain changes and reformations, came Rabindranath Tagore (d. 1941) and Mahatma Gandhi (d. 1948), who were extremely influential. Tagore made a rational, monistic interpretation of the *Upanisads*. Gandhi's teachings led to vast social change and the uplift of the backward and depressed Hindu castes. He stated that his whole religion is based on surrendering to God's will, the spirit of renunciation as embodied in the *Isa Upanisad*, the *Bhagavad Gita*, and the ideals of practical service. He gave a new interpretation to non-violence, which is as old as Hinduism, and tried to adapt it by means of *satyagraha* (passive resistance) to political and moral issues.

Gandhi sought to uplift the depressed and backward castes and to create a national entity. Speaking in Travancore on the Temple Entry Proclamation enacted there in 1936, he said:

> These temples are the visible symbols of God's power and authority. They are, therefore, truly called the houses of God, the houses of prayer. We go there in a prayerful mood and perform, first thing in the morning after ablution, the act of dedication and surrender. Now you can easily understand that, in the presence of God, the Ruler of the Universe, who pervades everything, even those whom we have called the lowest of the low, all are equal.[44]

Persia. Zoroastrianism, the indigenous religion of pre-Islamic Persia, was founded by Prophet Zarathushtra (d. 551 bce), known to the Greeks as Zoroaster. Zoroastrianism was the dominant regional religion during the Persian empires (559 bce to 651 bce), and was thus the most powerful religion at the time of Jesus. It had a major influence on other religions, and is still practiced today, especially in Iran and India.

According to Mary Boyce, Zoroaster believed that God had entrusted him with a message for humanity. He preached in plain words to ordinary people. His teachings were handed down orally and then written down under the Sassanids, rulers of the third Iranian empire (c.224 ce-c.640 ce). The language of that time was Middle Persian (Pahlavi). These books provide valuable keys

---

44 Much of this section was taken from http://www.uni-giessen.de.

for interpreting the obscurities of the Gathas (the hymns of Zarathustra) themselves.[45]

Moral values have a prominent place, and belief in an afterlife is a major creedal pillar. We quote below some sayings of Adhurbadh (son of Mahraspand) a Zoroastrian saint[46]:

- Do not hoard against the day when you may be in need.
- Strive to hoard up only righteousness, (that is) virtuous deeds, for of (all) the things that one may hoard, only righteousness is good.
- Do not harbor vengeance in your thoughts, lest your enemies catch up with you.
- Show moderation in your eating (and drinking) so that you may live long.
- Though a man be very poor in the goods of this world, he is (nevertheless) rich if there is moderation in his character.
- Pay more attention to your soul than to your belly, for one who fills his belly usually brings disorder on his spirit.
- Make the traveler welcome so that you yourself may receive a heartier welcome in this world and the next.
- Do not strive for (high) office, for the man who strives for (high) office usually brings disorder on his spirit.
- Live in harmony with virtue and do not consent to sin.
- Abstain rigorously from churlishness, self-will, enmity to the good, anger, rapine, calumny, and lying so that your body be not ill-famed and your soul damned.
- Do not plot evil against the evil, for the evil man reaps "the fruit of" his own bad actions.
- Do good simply because it is good. Do not do to others anything that does not seem good to yourself.
- Do not violently strike innocent people because you are angry with someone.
- Do not rejoice overmuch when good fortune attends you, and do not grieve overmuch when bad fortune overtakes you, for both good and bad fortune must befall man.

---

45 Mary Boyce, *Zoroastrians: Their Religious Beliefs and Practices*, London: 1979, p. 17.

46 J. D. Jamasp-Asana, ed., *Pahlavi Texts*, Bombay: 1897, pp. 144-53.

- Do not mock at anyone at all, for he who mocks himself becomes the object of mockery.
- Do not leave any sin for which penance is demanded (unconfessed) even for a moment so that the pure Religion of the worshippers of Ohrmazd may not be your enemy.
- The body is mortal, but the soul does not pass away.
- Do good, for the soul (really) is, not the body; spirit (really) is, not matter.
- Out of respect for the body do not neglect your soul; and do not, out of respect for anyone, forget that the things of this world are transitory. Desire nothing that will bring Penance on your body and punishment on your soul.

A journeying to Heaven and Hell. Arda Viraf was an important scholar of Zoroastrianism. His book narrates a vision of Heaven and Hell that he claimed to have seen in an inspired dream or vision.[47] It is truly Dantesque. We do not know its age, but we can say confidently that it is several centuries older than the work of Dante. The following passages give an idea about the Zoroastrian belief in afterlife.

> In the Name of God

> And the soul of Viraf went, from the body, to the Chinwad bridge of Chakat-i-Daitik, and came back the seventh day, and went into the body. Viraf rose up, as if he arose from a pleasant sleep, thinking of Vohuman and joyful... And he recounted the praises of Ohrmazd and the *archangels; and thanks to Hordad and Amurdad, the archangels*; and he muttered the benedictions (*afrinagan*).

> He directed thus: "Bring a writer who is wise and learned." And an accomplished writer, who was learned, was brought, and sat before him; and whatsoever Viraf said, he wrote correctly, clearly, and explicitly.

> And he ordered him to write thus:

> In that first night, Srosh the pious and Adar the angel came to meet me, and they bowed to me, and spoke thus: "Be thou welcome, Arda

---

47 Contained in Charles F. Horne, ed., *The Sacred Books and Early Literature of the East*, Vol. VII, Ancient Persia, 1917.

Viraf, although thou hast come when it is not thy time." I said: "I am a messenger." And then the victorious Srosh the pious, and Adar the angel, took hold of my hand. Taking the first footstep with the good thought, and the second footstep with the good word, and the third footstep with the good deed, I came up to the Chinwad bridge, the very wide and strong and created by Ohrmazd.

When I came up there, I saw a soul of the departed, whilst in those first three nights the soul was seated on the top of the body, and uttered those words of the Gatha: "*Ushta ahmai yahmai ushta kahmaichit*"; that is, "Well is he by whom that which is his benefit becomes the benefit of any one else." And in those three nights, as much benefit and comfort and enjoyment came to it, as all the benefit which it beheld in the world; just as a man who, whilst he was in the world, was more comfortable and happy and joyful through it.

In the third dawn, that soul of the pious departed into the sweet scent of trees; and he considered that scent which passed by his nose among the living; and the air of that fragrance comes from the more southern side, from the direction of God.

And there stood before him his own religion and his own deeds, in the graceful form of a damsel, as a beautiful appearance, that is, grown up in virtue; with prominent breasts, that is, her breasts swelled downward, which is charming to the heart and soul; whose form was as brilliant, as the sight of it was the more well-pleasing, the observation of it more desirable.

And the soul of the pious asked that damsel thus: "Who art thou? and what person art thou? than whom, in the world of the living, any damsel more elegant, and of more beautiful body than thine, was never seen by me."

To him replied she who was his own religion and his own deeds, thus: "I am thy actions, O youth of good thoughts, of good words, of good deeds, of good religion. It is on account of thy will and actions that I am as great and good and sweet-scented and triumphant and undistressed as appears to thee...."

And afterward, Srosh the pious, and Adar the angel, took hold of my hand, and said thus: "Come on, so that we may show unto thee heaven and hell; and the splendor and glory and ease and comfort and pleasure and joy and delight and gladness and fragrance which are the reward of the pious in heaven. We shall show thee the darkness and confinement and ingloriousness and misfortune and distress and evil and pain and sickness and dreadfulness and fearfulness and hurtfulness and stench in the punishments of hell, of various kinds, which the demons and sorcerers and sinners perform. We shall show thee the place of the true and that of the false."

I came to a place, and I saw the souls of several people, who remain in the same position. And I asked the victorious Srosh the pious, and Adar the angel, thus: "Who are they? and why remain they here?"

Srosh the pious, and Adar the angel, said thus: "They call this place *Hamestagan* (the ever-stationary); and they are the souls of those men whose good works and sin were equal. Speak out to the worlds thus: "Let not avarice and vexation prevent you from doing a very easy work, for every one whose good works are three *Srosho-charanam* more than his sin goes to heaven; they whose sin is more go to hell; they in whom both are equal remain among these Hamestagan till the future body." Their punishment is cold, or heat, from the revolution of the atmosphere; and they have no other adversity."

And afterward, I put forth the first footstep to the star track, on Humat, the place where good thoughts (*humat*) are received with hospitality. And I saw those souls of the pious whose radiance, which ever increased, was glittering as the stars; and their throne and seat were under the radiance, and splendid and full of glory.

And I asked Srosh the pious, and Adar the angel, thus: "Which place is this? and which people are these?"

Srosh the pious, and Adar the angel, said thus: "This place is the star track; and those are the souls who, in the world, offered no prayers, and chanted no Gathas, and contracted no next-of-kin marriage; they have also exercised no sovereignty, nor rulership nor chieftainship. Through other good works they have become pious."

I also saw the souls of those who, in the world, chanted the Gathas and used the prescribed prayers (*yeshts*), and were steadfast in the good religion of the Mazda-yasnians, which Ohrmazd taught to Zartosht;

when I advanced, they were in gold-embroidered and silver-embroidered clothes, the most embellished of all clothing. And it seem to me very sublime.

I also saw the souls of warriors, whose walk was in the supremest pleasure and joyfulness, and together with that of kings; and the well-made arms and equipments of those heroes were made of gold, studded with jewels, well-ornamented and all embroidered; and they were in wonderful trousers with much pomp and power and triumph. And it seemed to me sublime.

I came back again to the Chinwad bridge. And I saw a soul of those who were wicked, when in those first three nights so much mischief and evil were shown to their souls, as never such distress was seen by them in the world. And I inquired of Srosh the pious, and Adar the angel, thus: "Whose soul is this?"

Afterward, a stinking cold wind comes to meet him. So it seemed to that soul as if it came forth from the northern quarter, from the quarter of the demons, a more stinking wind than which he had not perceived in the world. And in that wind he saw his own religion and deeds as a profligate woman, naked, decayed, gapping, bandy-legged, lean-hipped, and unlimitedly spotted so that spot was joined to spot, like the most hideous, noxious creature (*khrafstar*), most filthy and most stinking.

Then that wicked soul spoke thus: "Who art thou, than whom I never saw any one of the creatures of Ohrmazd and Ahriman uglier, or filthier, or more stinking?"

To him she spoke thus: "I am thy bad actions, O youth of evil thoughts, of evil words, of evil deeds, of evil religion. It is on account of thy will and actions that I am hideous and vile, iniquitous and diseased, rotten and foul-smelling, unfortunate and distressed, as appears to thee."

Afterward, that soul of the wicked advanced the first footstep on Dush-humat and the second footstep on Dush-hukt, and the third on Dush-huvarsht; and with the fourth footstep he ran to hell.

I saw the soul of a man whom they ever forced to measure dust and ashes, with a bushel and gallon, and they ever gave it him to eat.

And I asked thus: "What sin was committed by this body, whose soul suffers such a punishment?"

Srosh the pious, and Adar the angel, said thus: "This is the soul of that wicked man who, in the world, kept no true bushel, nor gallons, nor weight, nor measure of length; he mixed water with wine, and put dust into grain, and sold them to the people at a high price; and stole and extorted something from the good."

I also saw the soul of a man who was held in the atmosphere, and fifty demons ever flogged him, before and behind, with darting serpents.

And I asked thus: "What sin was committed by this body, whose soul suffers such a punishment?"

Srosh the pious, and Adar the angel, said thus: "This is the soul of that wicked man who, in the world, was a bad ruler, and was unmerciful and destructive among men, and caused torment and punishment of various kinds."

I also saw the soul of a man whose tongue hung on the outside of his jaw, and was ever gnawed by noxious creatures (*khrafstars*).

And I asked thus: "What sin was committed by this body, whose soul suffers such a punishment?"

Srosh the pious, and Adar the angel, said thus: "This is the soul of that man who, in the world, committed slander, and embroiled people one with the other; and his soul, in the end, fled to hell."

I also saw the soul of a man whose tongue a worm ever gnawed.

And I asked thus: "What sin was committed by this body?"

Srosh the pious, and Adar the angel, said thus: "This is the soul of that wicked man who, in the world, spoke many lies and falsehoods; and, thereby, much harm and injury were diffused among all creatures."

Greece. Greek eschatology, as reflected in the Homeric poems, remains at a low level. Life on Earth, for all its shortcomings, is the highest good for people, and death the worst evil. Yet death is not extinction. The *psyche* survives, not the purely spiritual soul of later Greek and Christian thought, but an attenuated, semi-material ghost, shade, or image, of the earthly person. The life of this shade in the underworld is a dull, impoverished, almost functionless existence.

In later Greek thought on the future life, there are notable advances beyond the Homeric state, but it is doubtful whether the average popular faith ever reached a much higher level. Among early philosophers, Anaxagoras (d. c.428 bce) contributes to the notion of a purely spiritual soul.

A more directly religious contribution is made by the Eleusinian and Orphic mysteries, to the influence of which in brightening and moralizing the hope of a future life we have the concurrent witness of philosophers, poets, and historians. In the Orphic mysteries, the soul's divine origin and pre-existence, for which the body is but a temporary prison, and the doctrine of a retributive transmigration are more or less closely associated. It is hard to see how far the common belief of the people was influenced by these mysteries, but in poetical and philosophical literature their influence is unmistakable. This is seen especially in Pindar (d. c.438 bce) among the poets, and in Plato (d. 348 or 347 bce) among the philosophers.

Pindar has a definite promise of a future life of bliss for the good or the initiated—not merely for a few, but for all. Even the wicked who descend to Hades have hope. Having purged their wickedness they obtain rebirth on earth, and if, during three successive lives they prove themselves worthy of the boon, they will attain happiness in the Isles of the Blessed.

In Plato's teaching, the divine dignity, spirituality, and essential immortality of the soul being established, issues of the future for every soul are made clearly dependent on its moral conduct in the present life. There is a divine judgment after death, a heaven and a hell, and an intermediate state for penance and purification. Rewards and punishments are graduated according to the merits and demerits of each. The incurably wicked are condemned to everlasting punishment in Tartarus; the less wicked or indifferent also go to Tartarus or to the Acherusian Lake, but only for a time. Those who pursued goodness go to a happy home, the highest reward of all being for those who have purified themselves by philosophy.

JUDAISM AND CHRISTIANITY

The Judaic and Christian traditions can be summed up by giving the basic features of Old Testament eschatology.[48] They are the following:

- Old Testament eschatology, even in its earliest form, shares in the distinctive character of Old Testament religion generally. First, there are none of the erroneous ideas and tendencies that have a large place in ethnic religions. There is no pantheism, dualism, metempsychosis, or trace of Egyptian religious ideas or practices. It also stands apart from ethnic religions in its doctrine of God and of humanity in relation to God. Its doctrine of God is pure and uncompromising monotheism. The universe is ruled by the Wisdom, Justice, and Omnipotence of the one, true God. And humanity is created by God in His own image and likeness, and destined for relations of friendship and fellowship with Him.

- The Old Testament's stress the Divine Justice being exercised in this life has lead many to think that the Old Testament views religion mainly as an affair of this life, with retribution taking place on Earth.

To be fairly appreciated, however, this idea must be taken in conjunction with the national as opposed to the individual viewpoint. Allowance also must be made for its pedagogic value for the early Hebrews. Revelation and legislation had to be tempered for a singularly practical people, who were more effectively confirmed in God's worship and service by a vivid sense of His retributive providence on Earth than they would have been by a higher and fuller doctrine of future immortality with its postponement of moral rewards. This view gave a deep religious value and significance to every event of the present life, and raised morality above the narrow, utilitarian standpoint.

Worldly prosperity as such was not the ideal of the pious Israelite; rather, it was bestowed by God as a gracious reward for obeying His Commandments. This demonstrates another meaning and dimension when it is remembered that the Israelites were enslaved and persecuted

---

48 Mostly quoted from P. J. Toner, *The Catholic Encyclopedia*, Vol. V, "Judaic or Old-Testament Eschatology," Transcribed by Michael C. Tinkler.

by the Pharaohs. In order to reawaken them to the feeling of freedom and justice, drawing their attention to the importance of earthly life to realize the Divine just rule on Earth must have been provocative.

However, in subsequent revelations (e.g., the Psalms, Job, Isaiah, the Prophets, and Daniel) that came after their deliverance through Moses and the establishment of their kingdom, great stress was laid on the after-life, where the pious would be rewarded with eternal bliss and the wicked would be chastised. This was done to prevent the Israelites from indulg-ing in worldly life, ignoring the religious injunctions, and to divert their attention to the judgment that would take place in the next life. This is also why Jesus came to emphasize the spiritual dimension of religion and draw their attention to the other life.

- The Old Testament contains a national eschatology centered on the hope of establishing a theocratic and Messianic kingdom on Earth. However spiritually this idea may be expressed in the prophecies, the Jews mostly clung to a material and political interpretation of the kingdom, coupling their own domination with the triumph of God and the worldwide establishment of His rule.

There is much, indeed, to account for this in the obscurity of the proph-ecies themselves. However, the Messiah as a distinct person is not always mentioned in connection with the kingdom's inauguration. This leaves room for the expectation of a theophany of Yahweh (Jehovah) in the character of judge and ruler. Even when the Messiah's person and place are distinctly fore-shadowed, the fusion together in prophecy of what we have learned to distin-guish as his first and his second coming tends to give an eschatological charac-ter to the whole picture of the Messianic kingdom, when in reality it belongs only to its final stage. It is in such a way that the resurrection of the dead is introduced:

> But your dead will live; their bodies will rise. You who dwell in the dust, wake up and shout for joy. Your dew is the like of the dew of the morning; the earth will give birth to her dead. (Isaiah 26:19)
> Multitudes who sleep in the dust of the earth will awake: some to everlasting life, others to shame and everlasting contempt. (Daniel 12:2)[49]

---

49 Holy Bible, The Gideons, 1988.

- In the Psalms and the Book of Job, we find a clear expression of hope or assurance that just people will attain a life of blessedness after death. Here is voiced, under Divine inspiration, the innate craving of the righteous soul for everlasting fellowship with God, the protest of a strong and vivid faith against the popular conception of Sheol.[50] Omitting doubtful passages, it is enough to refer to Psalms 16, 17, 49, 50, and 73, which are clear enough to see that the good and pious will be eternally rewarded in another life, while the wicked and unjust be punished.

The same faith emerges in the Book of Job, first as a somewhat questionably expressed hope, and then as an assured conviction:

> If only You would hide me in the grave and conceal me till Your anger has passed! If only You would set me a time and then remember me! If a man dies, will he live again? All the days of my hard service I will wait for my renewal to come. You will call and I will answer You; You will long for the creature Your hands have made. (Job 14:13-14)

The hope gradually becomes more absolute and it takes the form of a definite certainty that he will see God, his Redeemer:

> I know that my Redeemer lives and that in the end He will stand upon the earth [dust]. And after my skin has been destroyed, yet in my flesh I will see God; I myself will see Him with my own eyes— I, and not another. How my heart yearns within me! (Job 19:23-27)

> As seen from these quoted verses, the Resurrection finds definite expression in subsequent revelations. It is clearly a personal resurrection that is taught.

Jewish apocryphal literature of the second and first centuries bce contains new eschatological developments that are mainly concerned with a more definite doctrine of retribution after death. Sheol is still most commonly understood as the general abode of the departed awaiting resurrection, an abode having different divisions to reward the righteous and punish the wicked. In reference to the latter, Sheol is sometimes simply equivalent to Hell. *Gehenna* is usually applied to the final place of punishment of the wicked after the last judgment, or even immediately after death; *paradise* is often used to designate the intermediate abode of the souls of the just, and heaven their home of final blessed-

---

50 The ancient Jewish land of the dead.

ness. Christ's use of these terms shows that the Jews of his day were sufficiently familiar with their New Testament meanings.

Eschatology in the New Testament. New Testament or Christian eschatology in general may be summed up in the following headings:

Death: Death, the separation of soul and body, is understood mainly as the consequence and penalty of Adam's sin (Romans 5:12). As the end of our probation, it decides our eternal destiny (II Corinthians 5:10; John 9:4; Luke 12:40, 16:19-31) but does not exclude an intermediate state of purification for the imperfect who die in God's grace. As a universal, though as to its absolute universality (for those living at the end of the world), there is some room for different commentary or form based on I Thessalonians 4:14-18 and I Corinthians 15:51.

The approach of the end of the world: Despite Christ's express refusal to specify when the world will end (Mark 13:32; Acts 1:6 sqq.), early Christians believed that it was near. This view seems to have been supported, at least partially, by some of Christ's sayings in reference to Jerusalem's destruction, which are set down in the Gospels side by side with prophecies relating to the end (Matthew 24; Luke 21), and in certain passages of the Apostolic writings. On the other hand, according to Matthew 24:14, Christ predicted that the Gospel would be preached to all nations before the end, and St. Paul looked forward to the ultimate conversion of Jews as a remote event preceded by that of the Gentiles (Romans 11:25 sqq.). Various events are spoken of as preceding or ushering in the end: a great apostasy (II Thessalonians 2:3 sqq.), a falling away from faith or charity, the reign of Antichrist, great social calamities, and terrifying physical convulsions. Yet the end will come unexpectedly (Luke 17, 18; Matthew 24).

Particular judgment: That a particular judgment of each soul takes place at death is implied in many New Testament passages (e.g., Luke 16:22 sqq., 23:43; Acts 1:25), and in the teaching of the Council of Florence regarding the speedy entry of each soul into heaven, purgatory, or hell.[51]

Heaven. Heaven is the abode of the blessed. There (after the resurrection with glorified bodies), Christians will enjoy, in the company of Christ and the angels, the immediate vision of God face to face, being supernaturally elevated by the light of glory to experience such a vision. There are infinite degrees of glory corresponding to degrees of merit, but all are unspeakably happy in the

---

51 Denzinger, *Enchiridion*, no. 588.

eternal possession of God. Only the perfectly pure and holy can enter heaven. For those who have attained that state, either at death or after purification in purgatory, entry into heaven is not deferred, as has sometimes been erroneously held, till after the General Judgment.

Purgatory. Purgatory is the intermediate state of unknown duration in which those who die imperfect, but not unrepentant of mortal sin, undergo purification to qualify for admission into heaven. They share in the communion of saints and are benefited by our prayers and good works. However, most non-Catholic denominations deny the existence of purgatory.

Hell. In Catholic teaching, Hell designates the place or state of human beings (and angels) who, because of sin, are excluded forever from the Beatific Vision. In this wide sense, it applies to those who die with only Original Sin on their souls.[52] This is not a state of misery or subjective punishment, but merely implies the objective privation of supernatural bliss, which is compatible with perfect natural happiness.

In the narrower sense in which this word is ordinarily used, Hell is the state of those who are punished eternally for unrepented personal mortal sin. Catholic doctrine does not go beyond affirming the existence of such a state, with varying degrees of punishment corresponding to degrees of guilt and its eternal duration. It is a terrible and mysterious truth, but is clearly and emphatically taught by Christ and the Apostles. Rationalists may deny its eternity despite Christ's authority, and those professing Christians unwilling to admit it may try to explain away Christ's words. However, according to Catholic teaching, it remains the divinely revealed solution to the problem of moral evil.

Rival solutions have been sought in some form of restitution or, less commonly, annihilation or conditional immortality. The restitutionist view, which in its Origenist form was condemned at the Council of Constantinople in 543 and later at the Fifth General Council, is the cardinal dogma of modern Universalism and is more or less favored by liberal Protestants and Anglicans. Annihilationists, on the other hand, believe that the finally impenitent will be annihilated or cease to exist.

THE RESURRECTION OF THE BODY

The visible coming of Christ in power and glory will be the signal for the rising of the dead. Catholic teaching states that all people will rise with the bodies they

---

52 Denzinger, Council of Florence, no. 588.

had in this life. But exactly what is required to constitute the identity of the risen and transformed body with the present body is not known. Though not formally defined, it is sufficiently certain that there will be only one simultaneous resurrection for the good and the bad.

The general judgment: Matthew 25 gives a general description of this event, which says that Jesus Christ will be the Judge on that day.

The consummation of all things: There is mention also of the physical universe sharing in the general consummation (II Peter 3:13; Romans 8:19 sqq). The present Heaven and Earth will be destroyed, and a new Heaven and Earth take their place. But what precisely this process will involve, or what purpose the renovated world will serve, are not revealed.

Pope John Paul II on the Catholic Christian eschatology: The following is an excerpt from Pope John Paul II's understanding of Catholic eschatology:

> Remember that at the end you will present yourself before God with your entire life. Before His judgment seat you will be responsible for all of your actions, you will be judged not only on your actions and on your words but also on your thoughts, even the most secret.
>
> Man is free and therefore *responsible.* His is a personal and social responsibility, a responsibility before God, a responsibility which is his greatness. I understand the fears of which you are speaking: you are afraid that the fact that one no longer speaks of these things in evangelization, in catechesis, and in homilies represents a *threat to this basic greatness of man.* Indeed, we could ask ourselves if the Church would still be able to awaken heroism and produce saints without proclaiming this message. And I am not speaking so much about the "great" saints, who are elevated to the honor of the altars, but of the "everyday" saints, to use the term in the sense it has had from early Christian literature.
>
> Significantly, the Council also reminds us of the universal call to holiness in the Church. This vocation is universal and concerns each of the baptized, every Christian. It is always very personal, connected to work, to one's profession. It is an account rendered of the talents each person has received—whether one has made good or bad use of them. We know that the words the Master Jesus spoke about the man who had buried the talent were very harsh and threatening (cf. *Mt* 25:25-30).

It can be said that until recently the Church's catechesis and preaching centered upon an *individual eschatology*, one, for that matter, which is profoundly rooted in Divine Revelation. The vision proposed by the Council, however, was that of an *eschatology of the Church and of the world.*

The title of chapter 7 of *Lumen Gentium*—"The Eschatological Nature of the Pilgrim Church"—which I suggested you reread, clearly reveals this intention. Here is the opening passage: "The Church, to which we are all called in Jesus Christ and in which through God's grace we attain holiness, will reach its fulfillment only in the glory of heaven, when the time comes for the renewal of all things (cf. *Acts* 3:21), and when the human race together with the entire world, which is intimately connected to man and through him arrives at its destiny, will be perfectly renewed in Christ. . . . And indeed Christ, when He rose up from the earth, drew all to Himself (cf. *Jn* 12:32); rising from the dead (cf. *Rm* 6:9) He instilled in the Apostles His animating Spirit, and through the Spirit built His Body which is the Church, the universal sacrament of salvation; seated at the right hand of the Father, He is continually at work in the world guiding men to the Church and through it uniting them more closely with Himself, and nourishing them with His own Body and Blood He gives them a share in His glorious life. Therefore, the promised renewal that we await is already begun in Christ. It is carried forward by the Holy Spirit and through the Spirit it continues in the Church, where the faith teaches us the meaning of our temporal life, while we finish, in the hope of future good, the work given to us in the world by the Father, and thus give fulfillment to our salvation (cf. *Phil* 2:12). The end of the age has already arrived (cf. *1 Cor* 10:11) and the world's renewal is irrevocably set—and in a certain real way it is even anticipated in this world. Already, on earth the Church is adorned with true, even if imperfect, holiness. But until there are new heavens and a new earth, in which justice resides (cf. *2 Pt* 3:10-13), the pilgrim Church, with its sacraments and institutions which belong to the present stage of history, carries the mark of this fleeting world, and lives among creation, which still groans and struggles, yearning for the appearance of the children of God (cf. *Rm* 8:19-22)" (*Lumen Gentium* 48).

In fact, *people of our time have become insensitive to the Last Things*. On the one hand, *secularization and secularism* promote this insensitivity and lead to a consumer mentality oriented toward the enjoyment of earthly goods. On the other hand, the *"hells on earth"* created in this century which is now drawing to a close have also contributed to this insensitivity. After the experience of concentration camps, gulags, bombings, not to mention natural catastrophes, can man possibly expect anything worse from this world, an even greater amount of humiliation and contempt? In a word, hell?

To a certain degree, eschatology has become irrelevant to contemporary man, especially in our civilization. Nonetheless, *faith in God, as Supreme Justice*, has not become irrelevant to man; the expectation remains that there is Someone who, in the end, will be able to speak the truth about the good and evil which man does, Someone able to reward the good and punish the bad. No one else but He is capable of doing it. People continue to have this awareness, which has survived in spite of the horrors of our century. "And so it is appointed that men die once, and then comes judgment" (cf. *Heb* 9:27).

Eschatology is not what will take place in the future, something happening only after earthly life is finished. *Eschatology has already begun with the coming of Christ.* The ultimate eschatological event was His redemptive Death and His Resurrection. This is the beginning of "a new heaven and a new earth" (cf. *Rev* 21:1). For everyone, life beyond death is connected with the affirmation: "I believe in the resurrection of the body," and then: "I believe in the forgiveness of sins and in life everlasting." This is *Christocentric eschatology*.

The problem of hell has always disturbed great thinkers in the Church, beginning with Origen and continuing in our time with Sergey Bulgakov and Hans Urs von Balthasar. In point of fact, the ancient councils rejected the theory of the *"final apocatastasis,"* according to which the world would be regenerated after destruction, and every creature would be saved; a theory which indirectly abolished hell. But the problem remains. Can God, who has loved man so much, permit the man who rejects Him to be condemned to eternal torment? And yet, the words of Christ are unequivocal. In Matthew's Gospel He speaks clearly of those who will go to eternal punishment (cf. *Mt* 25:46). Who will these be? The Church has never made any pronouncement in this regard. This is a mystery, truly inscrutable, which embraces the holiness of God and the conscience of man. The silence of the Church is, therefore, the only appropriate position for Christian faith. Even when Jesus says of Judas, the traitor, "It would be better for that man if he had never been born" (*Mt* 26:24), His words do not allude for certain to eternal damnation.

At the same time, however, there is something in man's moral conscience itself that rebels against any loss of this conviction: Is not God who is Love also ultimate Justice? Can He tolerate these terrible crimes, can they go unpunished? Isn't final punishment in some way necessary in order to reestablish moral equilibrium in the complex history of humanity? Is not hell in a certain sense the ultimate safeguard of man's moral conscience?

The Holy Scriptures include the concept of the *purifying fire.* The Eastern Church adopted it because it was biblical, while not receiving the Catholic doctrine on purgatory.

Besides the bull of Benedict XII from the fourteenth century, the *mystical works of Saint John of the Cross* offered me a very strong argument for purgatory. The "living flame of love," of which Saint John speaks, is above all a purifying fire. The mystical nights described by this great Doctor of the Church on the basis of his own experience correspond, in a certain sense, to purgatory. God makes man pass through such an interior purgatory of his sensual and spiritual nature in order to bring him into union with Himself. Here we do not find ourselves before a mere tribunal. We present ourselves before the power of Love itself.

Perhaps this is enough. Many theologians, in the East and the West, including contemporary theologians, have devoted their studies to the Last Things. The Church still has its eschatological awareness. It still leads man to eternal life. If the Church should cease to do so, it would cease being faithful to its vocation, to the New Covenant, which God has made with it in Jesus Christ.[53]

---

53 Pope John Paul II, *Crossing the Threshold of Hope*, Random House, 1995.

CHAPTER 7
ESCHATOLOGY IN ISLAM

ESCHATOLOGY IN ISLAM[54]

The main aspects of Islamic eschatology are similar to the Judaic-Christian tradition. Since they were derived from the same source and so originate from Divine Revelation, many common points can be found: for example, the invasion of the world shortly before the end of time by the barbarous Gog and Magog (Ya'juj and Ma'juj) tribes, the appearance of Dajjal (the Anti-Christ) and then a Messiah and/or Mahdi who will bring justice and order after global chaos, a global apostasy just before the world's destruction, Doomsday, Resurrection, the Supreme Judgment, the Bridge (*sirat*), and Paradise and Hell as the final abode of conscious beings. It can be said that except for differences in details or secondary matters, these basic elements are common to Islam, Christianity, and Judaism.

In this chapter, beginning with the "last things" before the world's overall destruction, we will summarize the events and stations of the Hereafter. Before analyzing this, it is necessary to explain the language of the main Islamic religious literature.

THE LANGUAGE OF THE DIVINE SCRIPTURES AND THE PROPHETIC TRADITIONS

The Qur'an decrees: *There is not a thing wet and dry but it is in a manifest Book* (6:59). The Qur'an contains everything, but not to the same degree, in the form of seeds, nuclei, summaries, principles, or signs. Things are explicit, implicit, allusive, vague, or suggestive. Each form is used to meet the Qur'an's purposes and the context's requirements.

The Qur'an pursues four main purposes: To expose and establish in human minds and hearts God's existence and Unity, Prophethood, bodily resurrection, and the worship of God and justice.

To realize its purposes, the Qur'an draws our attention to God's acts in the universe, His matchless art displayed through creation, the manifestations of His Names and Attributes, and the magnificent, perfect order and harmony in

---

54 Said Nursi, *The Words*, "5th Ray of the 25th Word"; Nursi, *The Letters*, "1st, 3rd, 10th, and 15th Letters."

existence. It also explains how to worship and please the Creator. It makes frequent mention of the other life, and explains how we can gain eternal happiness and be saved from eternal punishment. It mentions certain historical events, and lays down the rules of personal and social good conduct and morality as well as the principles of a happy, harmonious social life. It also gives news of important future events, especially those that will happen before the end of time. These have a prominent place in both the Qur'an and the Prophetic sayings.

The Qur'an is the last Divine Scripture and Prophet Muhammad is the final Prophet. Thus, both address all times, places, and levels of understanding. As the vast majority of people are always commoners, the Qur'an and the Prophet use a style and language that is understandable to such people in order to guide them to the truth and the Qur'an's basic purposes. Thus symbols, metaphors, allegories, comparisons, and parables requiring interpretation are quite common. *Those who are well-versed in knowledge* (3:7) know how to approach and benefit from the Qur'an and the Prophetic Traditions.

Another reason why the Qur'an does not concentrate on future events explicitly is that the whole point of religion is to examine and test the individual so that elevated and base spirits may be distinguished. Just as raw materials are fired to separate diamond and coal, gold and soil, Divine obligations test conscious beings and make them compete so that the precious "ore" in the "mine" of human potential may be separated from the dross.

Since the Qur'an was sent to perfect humanity through trial in this abode of testing and competition, it can only allude to future events that everyone will witness one day, and only opens the door to reason to a degree that proves its argument. If it mentioned them explicitly, the test would be meaningless. If the truth of Divine injunctions and Qur'anic and Prophetic predictions were clearly evident, everyone would have to affirm them, thereby rendering our God-given mental and spiritual faculties meaningless.

After this note, we may continue with brief mention of the last things:

The Dajjal (Antichrist). The Prophet mentioned two Antichrists: Dajjal, who will appear in the non-Muslim world, and Sufyan, who will appear in the Muslim world. Both beings are the greatest of all the Dajjals and Sufyans to appear in the world after the Prophet. Islamic sources report from the Prophet that more than 30 Dajjals will appear after him, and that the one or ones to emerge before the end of time will be the most harmful and destructive.

Another important point to stress is that the narrations of such beings are not exclusively about their persons. Rather, they are about the ideologies, committees, and systems they will establish in all aspects of life. There are many reports from Prophet Muhammad about the Antichrist, with different degrees of authenticity according to the principles of Hadith science. We will mention some of them with the explanations of Bediuzzaman Said Nursi:

> It is reported that the hands of the Sufyan will be holed, meaning that the Sufyan will be a prodigal one and encourage prodigality and dissipation.

Another report: *A terrible person will appear before the end of time and when he gets up one morning, he finds that on his forehead is inscribed: This is an infidel.* This means that the Sufyan will be an apostate and, in imitation of unbelievers, he will compel people to be dressed after the style of the non-Muslim world.

Another report: *The dictators to appear before the end of time, including especially the Dajjal and Sufyan, will have a false paradise and hell.* This means that during their time people will be addicted to amusement and worldly pleasures and the difference of income among social classes will increase with the consequence that there will be rebellions against governments. Therefore the places of pleasure and amusement and jails and similar places of torture will stand side by side.

Another report: *Before the end of time there will be left almost no one who worships God and mentions His Names as an act of worship.* This means that the places where God is worshipped and His Names are mentioned will be closed and the number of believing worshippers will considerably decrease. Another meaning of this report is that just before the destruction of the world God will take the souls of believers and the world will be destroyed upon the heads of unbelievers.

Another report: *Certain terrible persons to emerge before the end of time such as the Dajjal claim divinity and make people prostrate before themselves.* This means that such persons will derive their force mostly from atheistic and materialistic trends and suppose themselves to have godly power. Their statutes will be built and people will be forced to bow before them as a way of adoration.

Another report: *The dissipation and dissention to appear before the end of time will be so widespread and powerful that no one can control his or her carnal self against them.* This means the dissipated life will seduce too many people, who will indulge in it willingly. It is because of the frightening dimensions of the dissipation and pleasure-addiction to emerge before the end of time that, upon the order of the Prophet, almost all Muslims have taken refuge in God for 14 centuries from the dissention that the Dajjal will cause.

Another report: *The Sufyan will be a knowledgeable one and fascinate many scholars.* This means that although devoid of such means of power and reliance as kingdom, tribe, wealth and courage, the Sufyan will gain authority owing to his intriguing capacity and political genius. He bans religious education. Mostly because of attachment to life, many religious scholars and educationists support him and his regime.

Another report: *The first day of the Dajjal is equal to a year, while his second day to a month, his third day to a week and his forth day to an ordinary day.* This miraculous Prophetic tradition means that the Dajjal will appear in the north and proceed toward the south. As known, in the places near the North Pole a whole year consists of a day and night, each of which lasts 6 ordinary months. Coming toward the south, there are places where a day lasts 3 months and a month and a week respectively.

Another meaning is that both the Dajjal and the Sufyan will have four periods of rule: in the first period they will cause in a single year such great destruction that it can normally be made in 300 years. The destruction they will cause in each year of their second period will be equal to 30 years' destruction by others, and in one year of their third period they will make 7 years' destruction. Their fourth period will be normalized.

Another report: *When the Dajjal appears, everyone will hear him. He will have an extraordinary mount and travel throughout the world within 40 days.* This means that the Dajjal will appear when the means of communication and transportation develop as much as an event happening in one part of the world will be heard in other parts and traveling throughout the world within around 40 days is possible.

Gog and Magog. According to Qur'an 18:94-98 and 21:96, these are two barbarous tribes living in eastern Asia. Once before, a world-conqueror known in the Qur'an as Dhul-Qarnayn went as far as their lands and, to protect neighboring peoples from their attacks, built a formidable wall. When the time comes, they will surmount this wall and invade the civilized world.

The Mongols, who invaded the Muslim world and went as far as central Europe, were considered as Gog and Magog by the Muslims and Christians of that time. Having mentioned this interpretation, Said Nursi adds that a new invasion will come from the same direction. According to certain Prophetic Traditions, such great wars will break out that almost nine-tenths of humanity will perish.

The Mahdi and the Messiah. This is perhaps the most important element of the last things. Both Jews and Christians expect a Messiah toward the end of time, and regard his coming as the sign of the final, worldwide triumph for each.

Islamic sources mention both individuals. Shi'a Muslims give particular importance to the Mahdi, who they say is named Muhammad. He is the twelfth (and last) Imam of a series that began with 'Ali ibn Abi Talib, the Prophet's cousin and fourth caliph. The Mahdi disappeared when he was 74 years old, and will reappear when the world is full of injustice to restore justice.

The majority of Muslims regard the Mahdi as one who will come toward the end of time, when the Muslim world is defeated and all Islamic principles are under comprehensive attack. Together with the Messiah, the Mahdi will defend the principles of Islam against atheistic and materialistic trends and revive the religious life. He will end the dominion of both the Dajjal and the Sufyan.

According to certain contemporary thinkers and scholars, including Said Nursi, the Mahdi is not a single person, but rather the name of a global Islamic revival. It has three periods, each of which will be represented by a person and his group. Its leaders will be well-versed in religious sciences; have the highest moral standards; know the social, political, and economic conditions of their times; and be equipped with the necessary qualities of leadership. Together with his followers, the leader of the first period will defend Islamic principles against materialistic trends and expose them in an appropriate way. In the second period, the revived Islamic principles will gain ascendancy in many parts of the world, and Islamic life will experience a significant revival. The third period will see the global revival of religious life.

The third period most probably will follow the invasion of Gog and Magog, which will interrupt the second period. Christianity, according to the relevant Islamic sources, will be freed from borrowings from certain ancient religions and philosophies and draw closer to Islam. They will cooperate to repel the attacks of Gog and Magog and free the world from their invasion. Sciences will realize full development. Cities will be built in the sky, and it will be easy to travel there. Probably as a result of developments in genetics, one pomegranate will suffice for as many as twenty people, and its rind will provide shade for them. Wheat produced in a small house balcony will be enough to feed a family for a year.

The Messianic mission attributed to Jesus Christ. According to Prophet Muhammad, the promised Messiah is Jesus Christ. He will return and then follow and fully support the Mahdi. To better understand this significant issue, which has been the subject of polemics for centuries, and to clarify an important Islamic principle and remove certain misunderstandings, we will discuss this topic at some length.

Almost all early Muslims were subjected to severe persecution in Makka. They bore them patiently and never thought of retaliation, as the Qur'an ordered the Prophet to call unbelievers to the way of God with wisdom and fair preaching, advised him to repel evil with what was better, and to respond to his enemies' sins and faults with forbearance and forgiveness. Eventually, Makkan intolerance compelled the Muslims to abandon their homes and property and emigrate to Madina, where they could live according to their beliefs, and where Islam's full social and legal dimensions could evolve in peace. But Makkan hostility continued, and in Madina itself Muslims became targets of conspiracies hatched by the Hypocrites. Also, since the Helpers (native believers of Madina) willingly shared all that they had with the Emigrants, all Muslims suffered privation.

In such strained circumstances, God Almighty permitted them to fight their enemies, who had wronged and driven them from their homes unjustly. The Battle of Badr was the first major Muslim–Makkan confrontation. Although outnumbered, the believers won a great victory. Until then—if we do not accept the opinions of some Qur'anic interpreters that *Sura Muhammad,* which discusses how to treat prisoners of war, was revealed before *Surat al-Anfal*—no Divine commandment had been revealed about how to treat captives. The Muslims did not know whether they were to kill the enemy on the battlefield or take them as prisoners.

After the battle, the Prophet consulted his Companions, as he always did where there was no specific Divine commandment. Abu Bakr said: "O God's Messenger, they are your people. Even though they wronged you and the believers, you will win their hearts and cause their guidance if you forgive and please them." 'Umar said: "O God's Messenger, the captives are the leading figures of Makka. If we kill them, unbelief will no longer be able to recover to encounter us. Hand over to each Muslims his kin. Let 'Ali kill his brother 'Aqil. Let Abu Bakr kill his son 'Abd al-Rahman, and ....[so on]."

God's Messenger turned to Abu Bakr and said: "O Abu Bakr, you are like Prophet Abraham, who said: *He who follows me is of me, and he who disobeys me—but You are indeed Oft-Forgiving, Most Compassionate* (14:36). You are also like Jesus, who said: *If You punish them, they are Your servants. If You forgive them, You are the All-Mighty, the All-Wise* (5:118).

Then he turned to 'Umar and said: "O 'Umar, you are like Noah, who said: *O my Master, don't leave even a single unbeliever on the Earth!* (71:26) You are also like Moses, who said (of Pharaoh and his chieftains): *Our Master, destroy their riches and harden their hearts so that they will not believe until they see the painful chastisement* (10:88).

The episode illustrates an important aspect of human nature in relation to the mission of Prophethood and religion in humanity's life. A human being is a tripartite creation composed of spirit, carnal self, and body. These three elements are so closely interrelated that neglecting one makes it impossible to achieve perfection. Each human being thus has been endowed with three essential faculties: heart or spiritual intellect, reason, and will.

During a person's life, he or she experiences a continual inner struggle between good and evil, right and wrong. The motor of this struggle is the will, as directed by reason. However, as human reason can be swayed by carnal desire, personal feeling, interest, and such emotions as anger and rancor, it needs the spiritual intellect to guide it. The spiritual intellect, which includes the conscience, is the source of moral values and virtues.

Historically, divinely revealed religions have determined what is right and wrong on the authority of their Revealer (God) and of the character of the Prophets who conveyed the first Revelation.

Because of our worldly nature, we can be dominated by our lusts. When such people become rulers, they light fires of oppression and reduce the poor and the weak to slaves or servants. Human history is full of such instances. However, as God is All-Just and never approves of oppression, He sends His Prophets to guide and correct our individual and collective lives. All Prophets came with the same doctrine: belief in One God, Prophethood, Resurrection,

Angels, Divine Scriptures and Divine Destiny, worshipping God, and maintaining justice.

All Prophets conveyed the same moral principles. In this sense, all Divine religions are one and the same. However, varying cultural, geographical, social, and economic conditions require that different Prophets to be sent to each nation, and that the acts and forms of worship, as well as the law's subdivisions, differ slightly. This all ended with the sending of Prophet Muhammad and Islam, and so no more Prophets or revelations will ever be necessary.

There is an important point to be added here. When a Prophet passed away, his nation gradually would begin to alter some religious principles, borrow some polytheistic elements from pagan practices, and go astray, thus corrupting the Divine religion. This historical fact was another reason for the long series Prophets sent throughout history.

Islam, being the last and universal form of the Divine religion, orders its followers to believe in all Prophets. Being a Muslim also means being a follower of Jesus, Moses, and all other Prophets. The Qur'an declares:

> The Messenger (Muhammad) believes in what has been revealed to him by his Master, and so do the believers. They all believe in God and His angels, His Scriptures and His Messengers: "We make no distinction between any of His Messengers"—and they say: "We hear and obey. Grant us Your forgiveness, our Master; to You is the journeying." (2:285)

Due to their historical conditions, the messages of all previous Prophets were restricted to a certain people and period, and certain principles were given prominence. Also, God bestowed special favors on each Prophet and community according to the dictates of the time. For example, Adam was favored with knowledge of the "names" (the keys to all branches of knowledge); Noah was endowed with steadfastness and perseverance; Abraham was honored with intimate friendship with God and being the father of numerous Prophets; Moses was given the ability to administer and was exalted through being addressed directly by God; and Jesus was distinguished with patience, tolerance, and compassion.

Although each Prophet has some share in the praiseworthy qualities mentioned, each one surpasses, on account of his mission, the others in one or more of those qualities.

When Moses was raised as a Prophet, the Israelites were slaves to the Pharaohs, whose despotic and oppressive rule had ingrained slavery into their souls. To reform them, to equip them with such lofty feelings and values as freedom and independence, and to rebuild their character and free them, Moses came with a message containing stern and rigid rules and measures. This is why he was given the Torah, meaning Law. For the same reason, he was a somewhat unyielding and stern reformer and educator. Therefore, it was quite natural for him to pray in reference to Pharaoh and his chieftains: "Our Master, destroy their riches and harden their hearts so that they will not believe until they see the painful chastisement."

By Jesus' time, the Israelites had abandoned themselves to worldly pleasure and materialism. The Qur'an (9:34) states that the common people, as well as and even more so, the rabbis and scribes consumed the goods of others and barred people from God's way. They exploited religion for worldly advantage:

> You see many of them vying in sin and enmity and how they consume the unlawful; evil is the thing they have been doing. Why do the masters and rabbis not forbid them to utter sin, and consume the unlawful? Evil is the thing they have been doing. (5:62-63)

A similar, even severer, sentiment is to be found in the Gospels, attributed to Jesus:

> You snakes—how can you say good things when you are evil. For the mouth speaks what the heart is full of. A good person brings good things out of his treasure of good things; a bad person brings bad things out of his treasure of bad things. (Matthew 12:34-35)

> Take care: be on your guard against the yeast of the Pharisees and Sadducees. The teachers of the law and the Pharisees are the authorized interpreters of Moses' Law. So you must obey and follow everything they tell you to do; do not, however, imitate their actions, because they don't practice what they preach. They tie onto people's backs loads that are heavy and hard to carry, yet they aren't willing even to lift a finger to help them carry those loads. They do everything so that people will see them. They love the best places at feasts and the reserved seats in the synagogues; they love to be greeted with respect in the marketplaces and to have people call them "Teacher." (Matthew 23:1-7)

> ... How terrible for you, teachers of the Law and the Pharisees. You hypocrites. . . You give to God one tenth of the seasoning herbs, such as mint, dill and cumin, but you neglect to obey the really important teachings of the Law, such as justice and mercy and honesty. These you should practice, without neglecting the others. (Matthew)

When Jesus was sent to the Israelites, the spirit of religion had been reduced to a device used to rob the common people. So before putting the Law into effect, Jesus concentrated on faith, justice, mercy, humility, peace, love, repentance for one's sins, begging God's forgiveness, helping others, and purity of heart and intention and sincerity:

> Happy are those who know they are spiritually poor: The Kingdom of heaven belongs to them. Happy are those who mourn: God will comfort them. Happy are those who are humble: They will receive what God promised. Happy are those whose greatest desire is to do what God requires: God will satisfy them fully. Happy are those who are merciful to others: God will be merciful to them. Happy are the pure in heart: They will see God. (Matthew 5:3-10)

Prophet Muhammad has all the qualities mentioned above, except being the father of Prophets. Moreover, because of his mission's universality, he is like Moses (a warner who established a Law and fought his enemies) and like Jesus (a bringer of good news who preached mercy, forgiveness, helping others, altruism, humility, sincerity, purity of intention, and moral values of the highest degree).

We should remember that the Qur'an declares that God sent the Prophet as a mercy for creation. Islam presents God, before all other Attributes and Names, as All-Merciful the All-Compassionate, for this is how He mainly manifests Himself. Given this, His wrath and punishment are only used when necessary, and not essential to the same degree of Mercy.) In other words, people attract God's wrath through their sins and wrongdoing. But as God is All-Forgiving, He forgives most of His servants' sins: *Whatever misfortune befalls you, is for what your own hands have earned and for many (of them) He grants forgiveness* (42:30).

From the historical episode mentioned at the beginning of this section, Abu Bakr represented the "mission of Jesus" and 'Umar stood for the "mission of Moses." Since Islam must prevail to the end of time, it requires its followers to act, according to circumstances, sometimes as Moses and sometimes as Jesus.

The Messianic mission of Jesus Christ. The reliable books of hadith contain many sayings of the Prophet that Jesus will return before the end of time and practice the law of Islam. Although those Traditions have so far been interpreted in different ways, Fethullah Gülen interprets them to mean that before the end of time, Islam must manifest itself mostly in the dimension represented by Jesus. In other words, the main aspects of the Messengership of Jesus must be given prominence in preaching Islam.

These aspects consist of the following items:

• Jesus always traveled. He did not stay in one place, but preached his message on the move. Therefore to preach Islam, its missionaries must travel or emigrate from place to place. They must be *the repenters, the worshippers, the travelers, the bowers, the prostraters, the enjoiners of good and the forbidders of evil, and the observers of God's limits. For them there is good news* (9:112).

• Mercy, love, and forgiveness had first place in Jesus' mission. He was a bringer of good news. Therefore, those who have dedicated themselves to the cause of Islam must give prominence to these same things, never forgetting that the Prophet was sent as a mercy for all worlds and all creation. They must convey the good news to every place and call people to the way of God with wisdom and fair exhortation. They must never be repellent.

The world needs peace now more than ever. Most of our problems arise from excessive worldliness, scientific materialism, and the ruthless exploitation of nature. Other problems lie mainly in rebelling against Heaven and in destroying the equilibrium between humanity and the environment through modern materialism and our corrupt attitude toward humanity and religion. Most people are reluctant to perceive that peace is possible only through peace with the spiritual order. To be at peace with the Earth, one must be at peace with the spiritual dimension of one's existence, which is possible by being at peace with Heaven.

In the Qur'an, Jesus introduces himself as follows:

> I am indeed a servant of God … He has commanded me to pray and to give alms as long as I live. And He has made me dutiful to my mother and has not made me oppressive, wicked. (19:30-32)

This means, from the viewpoint of Jesus' promised mission, that children will not be dutiful to their parents. Therefore, Islam's missionaries, besides performing their prayers accurately and helping the poor and needy, must respect their parents and elders:

> Your Master has decreed that you worship none but Him, and that you show kindness to your parents. If either or both of them attain old age with you, (show no sign of impatience, and) do not even say 'uff' to them; nor rebuke them, but speak kind words to them. (17:23)

One of Jesus' miracles was healing diseases and reviving the dead, for life was very important in his message. The Qur'an attaches the same degree of importance to life, and regards one who kills someone else wrongly as the killer of humanity. On the other hand, one who saves someone else's life has saved humanity. So, those who have dedicated themselves to the cause of Islam must attach the utmost importance to life by trying to prevent wars and find cures for illnesses, and knowing that reviving a person spiritually is more important than healing diseases. The Qur'an declares: *O you who believe! Respond to God and the Messenger, when the Messenger calls you to that which will give you life* (8:24).

The final, worldwide apostasy and the destruction of the world. The unprecedented developments in science and technology will cause humanity to believe that it has so much knowledge and power that an authority above itself is no longer required or necessary. This will lead people to rebel against Heaven and indulge in debauchery to the extent that a worldwide apostasy will take place. Few believers will be left, and the unbelieving, rebellious forces will destroy the Ka'ba. This will mark the end of the world. God Almighty will gently take the souls of the believers. According to Said Nursi, as the result of a probable collision of a heavenly body with the Earth, the Earth will begin to rotate in the opposite direction and the sun will rise in the west. This is the final sign of the world's destruction. Some Qur'anic verses describe this destruction are as follows:

> When the sun is folded up, and when the stars fall, losing their luster; and when the mountains are moved; and when the ten-month pregnant camels are abandoned; and when the wild beasts are herded together; and when the seas are set boiling... (81:1-6)

> When the sky is rent asunder; and when the planets are dispersed; and when the oceans are poured forth; and when the graves are overturned, each soul will know what it has sent forward and what it has kept back. (82:1-5)

> When the Earth is shaken with its (final) earthquake, and the Earth yields up its burdens, and man says: "What is the matter with it?" That day it will proclaim its tidings, because your Master inspired it. That day mankind will come forth in scattered groups to be shown their deeds. Whoever does good an atom's weight shall see it then; and whoever does ill an atom's weight shall see it then. (99:1-8)

DEATH AND THE SPIRIT AFTER DEATH[55]

People have an intrinsic feeling of eternity. They feel imprisoned in the narrow confines of this world and always yearn for eternity. Whoever hearkens to their conscious nature will hear it pronouncing eternity over and over again. Even the whole universe cannot compensate them for their "hunger" for eternal life, for which they were created. Humanity's natural inclination toward eternal happiness comes from an objective reality: the existence of eternal life and the human desire for it.

What is death? The body is an instrument of the spirit, which governs and controls all of its members, cells, and minute particles. When the appointed hour comes, any illness or failure in the body's functions means an invitation to Azra'il, the Angel of Death. In reality, God causes people to die. However, so that people should not complain of this to Him, as many consider it disagreeable, God uses Azra'il as a veil in taking souls. Also, He puts illnesses or some calamities as veils between Azra'il and death so that people will not blame him for death.

Since Azra'il was created from light, like all other angels, he can be anywhere and in any form simultaneously. He also can do many tasks at the same time. Like the sun giving heat and light to all things while being present through its images in innumerable transparent objects, Azra'il can take millions of souls at the same moment.

However, Archangels like Gabriel, Michael, Israfil, and Azra'il have subordinates that resemble them and are under their supervision. When righteous people die, angels come to them with smiles and radiant faces. After that Azra'il comes, either by himself or with his subordinates charged with taking such souls from the bodies. Sometimes just a subordinate comes. The verses: *By those who pluck out violently; by those who draw out gently* (79:1-2) indicate that these angels are different from those tasked with removing the souls of the wicked. Such souls are plucked out violently, and so have a sour, frightened face at death.

At the time of death, windows usually are opened for righteous believers from their places in Paradise, or are shown the other-worldly forms of their good deeds and sayings. Prophet Muhammad stated that these souls are drawn out as gently as the flowing of water from a pitcher. Better than that, martyrs do not feel the agonies of death and do not know that they are dead; instead,

---

55 Fethullah Gülen, *The Essentials of the Islamic Faith*, Chapter 2.

they consider themselves to be transferred into a better world and enjoy perfect happiness.

Prophet Muhammad asked Jabir, whose father 'Abd Allah ibn Jahsh was martyred at Uhud:

> Do you know how God welcomed your father? He welcomed him in such an indescribable manner that neither eyes have seen it, nor ears heard it, nor minds conceived of it. Your father said: "O God, return me to the world so that I will explain to those left behind how pleasant martyrdom is." God replied: "There is no longer return. Life is lived only once. However, I'll inform them of the circumstances you are in," and He revealed: Never think of those slain in the way of God to be dead; rather they are alive and are provided in the Presence of their Master. (3:169)[56]

One dies how one lives. Those who live good, righteous lives have good deaths; those who lived wicked lives do not. However, this does not mean that the righteous die easily or that those who seem to die easily were righteous, for God sometimes uses severe death agonies to cleanse people of sin. The Prophet says that whatever evil happens to a believer causes some of his or her sins to be erased.

Prophet Muhammad, the most advanced in worshipping God, advised performing the prescribed prayers during one's death agony, as did 'Umar, the second caliph. Khalid ibn Walid, one of history's few invincible generals, asked those beside his death-bed to bring his sword and horse. Such people like 'Uthman, 'Ali, Hamza, and Mus'ab ibn 'Umayr dedicated themselves to Islam and died as martyrs; others led dissipated lives and died while drinking, gambling, or indulging in immoral sexual activities.

For righteous believers, death is not something to be feared. Although the body decomposes and seems to extinguish the light of life and destroy pleasures, in reality it is only a discharge from the heavy duties of worldly life, a changing of residence, a transferring of the body, an invitation to and the beginning of everlasting life. The world is continually enlivened through creation and predetermination, and continually stripped of life through other cycles of creation, determination, and wisdom. Plants and trees appear to die. But their seeds rotting underground do not die; instead, they undergo chemical processes that cause them to re-form and reappear as new plants and trees. Given this, the

---

56 Bayhaqi, *Dala'il al-Nubuwwa*, 3:298.

apparent death of their seeds is really the beginning of a new plant or tree, a new, more perfect and elaborate life.

If this is true of such simple life forms, how can it not be true for human beings? Was not humanity created for greater purposes than plants and trees? Death discharges us from this narrow worldly life, which becomes more of a burden as we age and become ill, and causes us to enter the infinitely wide circle of the Eternal, Beloved One's Mercy. There, we enjoy the everlasting company of our loved ones and the consolation of a happy, eternal life. In effect, our grave is like our mother's womb: we leave both places for a more perfect life in another world.

THE SPIRIT IN THE INTERMEDIATE WORLD

Following death, the spirits of those people whose lives were characterized by goodness, virtue, and refinement are wrapped in silk or silk-like substances and carried away by the angels charged with taking the spirit to God's Presence. While carrying the spirit of a good, righteous person through the Heavens and all inner dimensions of existence, angels in every station it passes welcome it and ask: "Whose spirit is this? How beautiful it is!" Its bearers introduce it with its most beautiful titles by which it was called while in the world, and answer: "This is the spirit of that one who, for example, prayed, fasted, gave alms, helped others, and bore all kinds of hardship for God's sake." Finally, God Almighty welcomes it and tells the angels: "Return it to the grave where its body is buried, so that Munkar and Nakir, the interrogating angels, can investigate it."

The spirits of evil people are treated with disdain everywhere they pass and then thrown back into the grave, away from the Presence of God Almighty.

Whatever evil happens to us in this world is, with the exceptions of Prophets, because of our sins. If we are sincere believers who sometimes cannot avoid sinning, God, out of His mercy, allows some misfortunes to befall us and thereby erases some of our sins. Or He may give us a hard death, so that still-unpardoned sins will be forgiven or so that we may attain higher (spiritual) ranks, but then take our spirits very gently. If we still have some unforgiven sins after this, we will undergo some sort of punishment in the grave and then be spared any punishment of Hell. Since the grave is the first station toward eternal life, almost everyone except the Prophets will be interrogated by the two above-mentioned angels and subjected to some suffering.

As recorded in reliable Tradition books, 'Abbas, the Prophet's uncle, desired very much to see 'Umar in a dream after the latter's death. When he finally saw him in a dream 6 months later, he asked him: "Where were you until now?" 'Umar answered: "Don't ask! I have just finished accounting (for my life)."

Sa'd ibn Mu'adh was one of the greatest Companions. When he died, Gabriel told the Messenger: "The Divine Throne trembled due to Sa'd's death, O God's Messenger!" Innumerable angels took part in his funeral. However, after Sa'd was buried, the Messenger spoke in amazement: "Glory be to God! What (will happen to others) if the grave (even) squeezes Sa'd?"

In the grave, Munkar and Nakir ask each soul: "Who is your Master? Who is your Prophet? What is your religion, etc." Those who died as believers in God and the Prophet and Islam can answer these questions. Those who died as unbelievers cannot. Then the person's deeds are questioned.

Spirits interact with the body differently, for this relationship depends upon which world they inhabit. In this world, the spirit is confined within the "prison" of the body. If the carnal self and bodily desires dominate it, the spirit inevitably deteriorates and the person is doomed. If the spirit disciplines the carnal self through belief, worship, and good conduct and frees itself from servitude to bodily desires, it becomes refined and acquires purity and laudable qualities. This will bring it happiness in both worlds.

After burial, the spirit is kept waiting in the intermediate world. Although the body decomposes and rots away into the ground, its essential particles (or atoms) do not. One hadith call this part the *ajb al-dhanab* (coccyx). It might be a person's genes. But whatever it is, the spirit continues its relations with the body through it, as it is a foundation upon which God will resurrect each individual. God will make this part and its contents suitable for eternal life during the final destruction and rebuilding of the universe.

The intermediate world is the realm where spirits feel the "breath" of the bliss of Paradise or the punishment of Hell. If they led virtuous lives, their good deeds will appear to them as amiable fellows. Also, windows will be opened onto heavenly scenes and, as stated in a hadith, the grave will be like a garden of Paradise. However, those with unpardoned sins will have to undergo some sort of suffering in the intermediate world until their sins are purged and they are worthy of Paradise. Unbelievers and wicked people will meet their evil deeds in the form of bad fellows and vermin. They will see scenes of Hell, and the grave will be like one of Hell's pits.

While we live in the world, it is our spirit that suffers pain and feels joy and happiness. Although the spirit feels pain apparently through the nervous system and then uses it to communicate with all parts of the body, science still does not understand the spirit–body interaction, especially the role of the brain. Any failure in any part of the body can render the nervous system inoperative.

Science has established that certain brain cells continue to live for a while after death. Scientists have tried to receive signals through those cells. If they manage to receive and decipher those signals, the field of criminology will receive a great boost. The following verses give us an example of this. During the time of Moses, God revived a murdered one, who told the murderer:

> When Moses said to his people: "God commands you to sacri-
> fice a cow," ... they sacrificed her, a thing they had scarcely done.
> You had killed a living soul, and disputed thereon—God would
> disclose what you were hiding—so We said: "Smite him with part
> of it [the cow];" even so He brings to life the dead, and He shows
> you His signs, that haply you may have understanding. (2:67,
> 72-73)

Since the spirit and the body live the worldly life together and shares all its joys and pains, God will resurrect people bodily and spiritually. The Ahl al-Sunna wa al-Jam'a (the great majority of Muslims who follow the way of the Prophet and his Companions) agree that the spirit and the body will go to either Paradise or Hell together. God will build bodies in forms specific to the Hereafter, where everything will be alive: *This life of the world is but a pastime and a game, but the home of the Hereafter, that is life if they but knew* (29:64).

SENDING GIFTS TO THE SPIRIT AFTER DEATH

Spirits in the intermediate world will see and hear us, if God allows this. He may permit some saintly people to see, hear, and communicate with certain still-living people, or allow some of them to help us.

After we die, our record of deeds remains open if we have left behind good, virtuous children, books, or institutions that continue to benefit others. If we have raised or helped to raise people who benefit humanity, our reward increases; if we leave behind that which is evil, our sins increase for as long as they continue to harm people. So, if we want to help our loved ones in the intermediate world, we should be good heirs. By helping the poor, observing the rules of Islam, leading a good and virtuous life, and especially by spending to promote Islam, general Muslim well-being, and helping humanity, their reward will increase.

Necromancy is widespread among those seeking spiritual contentment. Great saints like Muhy al-Din ibn al-'Arabi communicated with spirits of the dead and the unborn.[57] Present-day spiritualists communicate not with the spirits of the dead, but with the unbelieving jinn or devils who assume the deceased's form. Also, those who predict future events usually contact jinn and then relate what they are told.

Jinn live longer than us, are active in broader dimensions (realms) of time and space, act much quicker, and can see some things we cannot. However, as they cannot see the future, we should not believe their predictions even though, very rarely, they may be correct.

We know that the American and Soviet intelligence agencies competed with each other for many years in such supernormal ways of communication as telepathy. As will be explained later, in the not too distant future, world powers will use jinn to communicate and gather intelligence. However, it is dangerous to seek to seek such contact and communication, for they can bring such people under their influence easily and govern their actions.

A psychiatrist friend of mine relates:

> I was invited to a practice of necromancy in a house in Samsun (a province in northern Turkey). The youngest daughter of the family arranged cups and letters on a table. One of the friends present invited the soul of his late grandfather. After several calls, a man appeared. When we asked him insistently who he was, he answered: "Satan."

> We were greatly astonished. A while later, I asked him why he had come although we had not called him. He wrote on the table with the cups: "So I come!" I asked him whether he believed in God. He wrote "No!" When I asked whether he believed in the Prophet, again, he wrote "No!"

> I began reading to him some passages from a book concerning the existence of God. When I read, "A factory with such and such features points to the engineer who planned and built it," he wrote "True"; but

---

57 The souls of all human beings were created long before the first human being existed. A person receives a soul when he or she is about a 6-week old embryo in the mother's womb.

when I read "So too the universe with all the planets and particularly the world with all plants and animals in it indicate God," he wrote "No!"

This continued for some time, and I began reciting to him from *Jawshan al-Kabir* (the "Great Armor"), a collection of supplications to God. While I was reciting, the cups were moving on the table. Meantime he wrote: "Give up that nonsense!" When I continued to recite, he could not endure listening and disappeared.

Since seeking this type of communication is risky, those who cannot distinguish between the spirit and jinn or devils, and who cannot protect themselves against their harm, should not pursue it.

CHAPTER 8
QUESTIONS

QUESTIONS

QUESTION: Are there degrees of life?[58]

ANSWER: Except for the eternal life in the other world, there are five degrees of life. The *first degree* is as we live here and now, which is bound by certain conditions.

The *second degree* is manifested in the lives of Khidr[59] and Elijah. To some extent it is free, for those who have it can be present in different places at the same time and are not bound by the necessities of ordinary human life. Like us they may eat and drink, but they do not really need to. The experiences with Khidr of some godly people, who can discern hidden truths, illuminate and prove this degree of life. Furthermore, one spiritual station that saints reach in their spiritual journey is "the station of Khidr." A saint who attains this station may meet Khidr and be directly instructed by him. Sometimes one who holds this station is even mistaken for Khidr himself.

The *third degree* is manifested in the lives of Prophets Jesus and Enoch. They live in Heaven free of any human necessity. Their physical bodies have acquired some sort of refinement and luminosity. Prophet Muhammad is reported to have said: "Jesus will come back to the world before the end of time and follow the Shari'a of Muhammad." This hadith *implies* that Christianity will be purified of certain elements and ultimately will work hand-in-hand with Islam. Both religions will use the "sword of Revelation" to eradicate the disbelief and materialism established by natural philosophy.

The *fourth degree* is the life of martyrs. Some Qur'anic verses state explicitly that martyrs enjoy a higher degree of life than non-martyrs. Since martyrs sacrifice their lives in His way, God Almighty grants them an intermediate life that resembles the worldly life, but without its pains and troubles. As martyrs do not feel the pangs of death, they do not even know that they are dead; rather, they consider themselves to be transferred to a better world and enjoy perfect happiness. The dead, however, know that they are dead, although their spirits

---

58 Said Nursi, *The Letters*, "1st Letter."

59 Khidr: One of the prophets whose name is mentioned in the Qur'an (37:123-130), Elijah (or Elias), peace be upon him, lived in the ninth century BC and came to revive the faith and law of Moses among the people of Israel. It is reported that he was raised to a different level of life and he meets with Khidr every pilgrimage season (see Nursi, *The Letters*, The First Letter).

are eternal. Also, the pleasure they experience in the intermediate life is less than that enjoyed by martyrs.

The difference can be explained by this analogy: In a dream, two people enter a palace as beautiful as Paradise. One is aware that this dream will disappear upon awakening and receives little pleasure. The other one does not know that this is a dream, and therefore is wholly contented and happy. Several Qur'anic verses and Prophetic Traditions, as well as the experience of countless people, prove that martyrs lead a life with some degree of consciousness and know that they are alive.

The *fifth degree* is the spiritual life of the dead. Death is a changing of residence, a discharge from worldly duties that frees the spirit. It is not nonexistence. This degree of life is proven by such repeatedly observed facts as the spirits of godly people appearing in their human (material) forms, and being seen by people who have insight into hidden truths. That the dead can communicate with us in dreams or even while we are awake is another proof.

QUESTION: What does the verse: *Your creation and your resurrection are as but a single soul* (31:28) mean?[60]

ANSWER: That the Divine Power can create and resurrect humanity as easily as it creates and resurrects one person. For example, by virtue of being a light-giving object, the sun is reflected with the same ease in all transparent things. Its reflection in one thing does not hinder its reflection in another. Due to its transparent nature, the tiniest transparent thing is equal to the ocean's vast face in containing the sun's image.

Another example is that a "natural" law prevalent in one member of a species is simultaneously prevalent in the species as a whole. Thus, the law of growth in living things is exercised at the same time, and with the same power and results, in all living beings. One's growth does not hinder that of another. This is so because:

- Pervasive orderliness and the interrelation of its parts mean that a child could steer a huge battleship as easily as a toy boat. These two facts also characterize creation, which means that the Divine Power can operate simultaneously in each part of creation, as well as the whole of creation, with the same ease.

---

60 Said Nursi, *The Words*, "10th Word" and "29th Word."

- Obedience allows a commander to ensure that when the command to march is given, both the entire army and the individual soldier will obey.

- If a set of scales could weigh two walnuts or two suns in its pans, we would see the following: If two suns or walnuts of equal weight were weighed, the same power of equilibrium would move the suns with the same ease as it moves the walnuts.

In our world, the existence of such qualities as luminosity and transparency, orderliness and interrelatedness, obedience and balance or equilibrium means that the largest and the tiniest things become equal, that many things appear equal to one thing. A light-giving object like the sun can operate simultaneously in the tiniest object and on the whole planet with the same ease. An immaterial "natural" law can operate in each member of a species at the same time.

The Absolutely Powerful One's Power is perfect, immaterial, and infinite. He will resurrect the dead with a single trumpet blast, as if they were a single human being, when the exact universal order dictated by Divine Wisdom and Destiny, everything's perfect obedience to His rule and operations, and the universe's exact balance and interrelatedness are joined with the transparency of the inner dimension of things.

Furthermore, degrees of strength and weakness are determined by the intervention of opposites. For example, degrees of heat are determined by the intervention of cold, degrees of beauty by the intervention of ugliness, and degrees of illumination by the intervention of darkness. But if a quality or property is essential to something, originates directly from itself and is almost identical with it, and so is not accidental to it, its opposite cannot intervene.

This assertion is based on the fact that opposites of the same qualities cannot be united in a single thing. Given that the Power of the Absolutely Powerful One is essential to His Divine Essence, directly originates from it and is almost identical with it, and that it is perfect, it cannot have an opposite to intervene in it. Hence, creating spring is as easy for the Master of Majesty as creating a flower. If attributed to material causes, creating a flower would be as hard as creating spring. By this analogy, it is as easy for the Master of Majesty to resurrect and assemble all of the dead as it is for Him to resurrect a single person.

QUESTION: Such verses as: *It is but a single cry* (36:53), which is often repeated, and *The command of the Hour is but a twinkling of the eye, or nearer*

(16:77), show that the Resurrection will happen in a single instant, without the passage of time. How are we to understand this?[61]

Answer: There are three elements [or stages, if time were not excluded] of the Resurrection: Spirits will return to their bodies, bodies will be reanimated, and bodies will be rebuilt and resurrected.

The first element. The dispersed soldiers of a highly disciplined army can be summoned together by a loud bugle blast. Israfil's trumpet is certainly more powerful than a bugle, and the spirits of human beings are more obedient, disciplined, and submissive than soldiers. They were in the Realm of Spirits before the universe's creation. When it is the time for a soul to be "breathed" into its body, it comes to the world. After death, people will be resurrected as if they were dispersed soldiers ordered to reform the army.

The second element. When a great city celebrates something, 100,000 lights can be turned on in a single instant by a switch in the city's power station. No time really passes. This could be done on a planetary scale if such a power station existed. If electricity, a creation of the All-Mighty that has been trained and disciplined by its Creator to manifest this property here, can do such a thing, then the Resurrection can occur in a twinkling of the eye within the framework of the orderly laws of Divine Wisdom.

The third element. There are thousands of analogies for the rebuilding and resurrection of human bodies. For instance, consider how tree leaves are perfectly restored, almost identically to those of last year, within a few days after spring begins, even though there are far more trees than people. Consider how all flowers and fruits are re-created just like those of last spring; the sudden awakening, unfolding, and coming to life of countless seeds, kernels, and roots that are the origin of spring growth; how trees, resembling upright skeletons, abruptly begin to show signs of "resurrection after death." And what about the reanimation of countless small creatures, especially the "resurrection" of flies, which occurs in just a few days every spring, along with other insects who vastly outnumber all human beings who have ever lived?

This world is the realm of Wisdom, for everything occurs within the framework of certain laws and gradually. The Hereafter is the abode of Power, wherein the Divine Power operates directly and without any law. Therefore, in this world and in accordance with the requirements of such Divine Names as All-Wise, Arranger, Disposer, Nurturer, and Trainer, creation is to some extent

---

61 ibid., "10th Word."

graduated over time. This is required by His Wisdom as Master and Sustainer. But in the Hereafter, Power and Mercy are more evident than Wisdom. As a result, creation is instantaneous and not limited by substance, matter, space, or time. The Qur'an decrees that what takes time here will be accomplished in an instant in the Hereafter: *The command of the Hour is but a twinkling of the eye, or nearer.*

If there is another element of the Resurrection, it is this world's destruction. If God allows a planet or asteroid to collide with our temporary home, it will be destroyed instantly, just as a palace built over a period of 10 years can be destroyed in a minute.

QUESTION: Will souls that have gained permanence through death be influenced by the events of Doomsday?[62]

ANSWER: They will be influenced according to their ranks, just as angels are influenced by the destruction of sinners when God's Wrath is demonstrated. As the human mind and spirit in a hot room are influenced by seeing someone trembling outside in the cold, so the conscious souls that have passed into eternity will be affected by the important events of the universe. This relationship is indicated in the Qur'an. The people of torment will be affected by their agony, while the people of happiness will be affected by their wonder and amazement, and even their joyful expectation of the coming of the final, endless bliss.

In many verses, the Qur'an says that humanity (and jinn) will be affected by the shock of these events, and emphasizes that everyone will experience them. But as only those alive at that time will experience it physically. Those spirits who no longer are joined to physical bodies also are encompassed, to some extent, within this Qur'anic verse.

QUESTION: Is *All things perish, except His "Face"* (28:88) also related to Paradise, Hell, and their inhabitants?[63]

ANSWER: This matter has been discussed by scholars, saints, and people of deep perception and insight. Some say that the people of the permanent world are not included in the meaning of this verse; others say that such people will be annihilated, but for such a short time that they will not feel this instant of perishing. Some who discover "hidden" truths claim that everything but God will permanently perish. However, this is not compatible with truth, for the

---

62 Said Nursi, *The Letters*, "15th Letter."
63 ibid.

Divine Essence and God's Attributes and Names are permanent. As the permanent beings in the permanent world are manifestations of those permanent Attributes and Names, and the mirrors in which they are reflected, they cannot be non-existent.

Consider the following points:

• As the All-Mighty is Omnipotent, creation and destruction are equally easy for Him. He can annihilate and resurrect creation in an instant. In addition, there is no such entity as "absolute non-existence," for His knowledge is all-encompassing. In other words, everything is contained or has a kind of existence or an ideal form within His infinite Divine Knowledge. Thus there is no room for "non-existence."

As for the "relative non-existence" within the encompassing circle of Divine Knowledge, essentially it is a nominal veil where the manifestations of Divine Knowledge are reflected. Some people of profound understanding call these "ideal" forms of existence "archetypes." For them, passing into non-existence means shedding an outer garment (the body) and returning to the circle of spiritual existence for a fixed time.

• Everything's existence depends on God, for everything exists only as a manifestation of the permanent Divine Names. Therefore, everything has a permanent, sublime reality. The verse: *All things perish, except His Face* also serves as a sword to liberate humanity from whatever is not God (e.g., the world, desire, and the vanities of life). Thus, whatever we have or do for the sake of God is not included here and so is not subject to perishing.

In sum, if we do everything only for His sake, none of these deeds will be included in the meaning of this verse. If we want to eternalize our deeds and be rewarded with permanent happiness, we must seek God and spend our lives for His sake and pleasure.

QUESTION: How will the Plain of Resurrection and Gathering be built? How will we be gathered there? Will we be naked? How will we meet our friends and find God's Messenger? How will God's Messenger meet countless people personally? How will the people of Paradise and Hell be clothed?[64]

ANSWER: As these questions are answered very clearly in the books of hadith, I will only mention a few points:

---

64 ibid., "28th Letter."

- The Earth follows a huge annual orbit and empties into the tablets of that circle, on an annual basis, the immaterial outcome and consequences of what has happened on it throughout the year. On the Day of Judgment, its whole life will assume a form specific to the Hereafter. On the Last Day, the Earth will submit the minor hell in its center to the major one (for the minor and major hells, see the question below: *Where is Hell?*). In addition, it will empty its contents into the Plain of Resurrection and Gathering, which will be built on its annual orbit.

- Just as a sun can be present, by virtue of being a luminary body, everywhere at the same time, God's Messenger, through his spirit's luminosity, can be present at the same time in thousands of different places and meet millions of people.

- God Almighty provides every creature, except humanity, with a natural covering. So, as a requirement of His being All-Wise, He will provide a "natural" covering in the Plain of Resurrection and Gathering for humanity. We wear artificial clothes here to protect ourselves from the cold and heat, for the sake of modesty, and to show our commanding position and power over other species. If this were not the case, we would be clothed quite simply. Without this wisdom of requiring humanity to be clothed somewhat elaborately, individuals dressed in rags would be ridiculed by other conscious beings. However, since this wisdom will not be sought in the Plain of Resurrection and Gathering, there will be no need for artificial clothing.

- An individual desires to receive, all at once, uninterrupted pleasure from every section of Paradise. Paradise has innumerable kinds of beauties that provide such pleasure. Thus, its inhabitants clothe themselves in specimens of those beauties, each becoming a miniature Paradise. Just as a gardener grows flowers, a shopkeeper lists merchandise, a carpenter makes furniture out of the material at hand, the people of Paradise will be dressed by God's Mercy. Their garments will show the beauties of Paradise in a way that pleases each sense and feeling, and satisfies each faculty.

This will be especially true for those who worshipped God in the world with all their senses and faculties, and therefore deserve all the pleasures of Paradise. Such garments will not be the same; rather, each one is of a different level to please senses and feelings, and has different particular beauties. In accordance with wisdom and justice, since the people of Hell committed many sins in the world, they will be clothed with different types of garments, each of which will cause them to suffer a special torment and resemble a miniature Hell.

QUESTION: Paradise and Hell are quite a long way from us. If the people of Paradise will fly across the Plain of Resurrection and Gathering into Paradise at the speed of light, how will the people of Hell, weighed down by the burden of their sins, reach their destination?[65]

ANSWER: Imagine that all nations were invited to a meeting on the other side of the Earth. Each would go there on a large ship of its own. Likewise the Earth, which already travels across the great "ocean" of the universe at a high speed, will convey its inhabitants to the Plain of Resurrection and Gathering on Judgment Day.

Besides, the Earth's center contains a fire of 200,000°C—which is the degree also mentioned in a Prophetic saying—given that heat increases by 1°C for every 33 meters toward the planet's center. The Earth's radius is 6,000 kilometers. This fire, as stated in some Traditions, fulfills in this world and the intermediate one some of Hell's functions, and will be discharged into Hell by the Earth. After this, the Earth will be changed into its permanent form, much more beautiful than its present one, and will be a station in the other world.

The Almighty Creator, One and All-Wise, accomplishes many things out of a few and uses a small thing to perform many tasks. This manifests His Power's perfection and His Wisdom's beauty, and proves His Oneness. Attributing everything to One Being makes everything so easy that it becomes virtually necessary.

When everything is attributed to various makers and causes, the ensuing difficulties make everything impossible. Can an army commander achieve any great results if his soldiers decide what they will and will not do? Can an architect construct anything really beautiful and worthwhile if his or her material could somehow decide upon how and where they would be used? The ensuing results would be graphic displays of difficulty and confusion.

If the movement of celestial bodies and the circulation of all things, all for the glorification of God, and the alternation of seasons and day and night are ascribed to One God, we can see that God, by causing a planet to move with a single order, demonstrates amazing instances of art in the succession of sea-

---

65 ibid., "3rd Letter."

sons, particular instances of wisdom in the alternation of day and night, and charming scenes in the apparent movements of the stars, sun, and moon. For *His is the gathering of all hosts* (48:7).

If He wills, He can place the Earth, which is insignificant when compared to other planets and galaxies, in the commanding position over all stars, and make the huge sun a lamp for its inhabitants. He also weaves matchless scenes of beauty, pictures of His Power's works, by using the four seasons as a shuttle. He uses day and night (pages of the Book of Wisdom) to divide and measure time and, by showing the moon every day in a different fashion, establishes lunar months.

Further, He makes the stars ornamented, elegant, charming, and shining lamps in the hands of angels whirling in ecstasy, thus displaying many instances of wisdom in connection with the relationship between the Earth and stars. If all these activities were not the work of a Being Who has absolute rule over all creation, then the Earth, moon, sun and all stars would have to perform every day a real, conscious movement in an endless circle and at an infinite speed.

Thus, because there is infinite ease in unity and in becoming one, and infinite hardship in multitude and division, those involved in crafts and trade give a form of unity to multitude by forming corporations to facilitate their business. In sum, there is infinite hardship in the way of misguidance, and infinite ease in the way of unity and guidance.

QUESTION: Where is the Plain of Resurrection and Gathering?[66]

ANSWER: *Say: "The Knowledge is with God"* (67:26). The sublime wisdom that the Wise Creator displays in everything also is manifested in the Earth's revolution. Its movement is not aimless; rather, it draws the periphery of a huge circle into which it continually empties the outcomes of all events happening upon it. On the Day of Judgment, the outcome of everyone's lives will be displayed.

According to a Prophetic Tradition, this huge circle will be centered on the area of Damascus, but in its expanded form and in accordance with the Hereafter's dimensions. The outcome of all events on the Earth is continually transferred to the registers or tablets of the Plain of Resurrection and Gathering. Presently, the Plain is behind the veil of the Unseen. However, we will see it on the Day of Judgment, as we will have assumed our Hereafter-specific forms.

---

66 ibid., "10th Letter."

The Earth is a field (of seeds to grow and be harvested for the Mustering), a stream (carrying our deeds forward), a measure of grain, a bushel (measuring and emptying the outcome of our deeds). By the end of time, enough deeds will have produced to fill up that great Plain. The Earth functions as a seed; this Plain and all its contents will grow from it, just like a tree. Just as a radiant dot becomes a radiant circle when spun quickly, God uses the rapid and purposeful movement of the Earth (a small dot compared to the universe), as well as the outcomes of its inhabitants, to form this Plain. *Say: "Surely, the true knowledge is with God."*

QUESTION: Where is Hell?[67]

ANSWER: *Say: "Knowledge is only with God"* (6:59). As belief and good conduct bear the seed of a sort of Paradise experienced by the spirit, unbelief and evil deeds contain the seed of a sort of Hell experienced spiritually. Unbelief and evil conduct are the seeds of Hell, and Hell is a fruit of unbelief, evil conduct, and wrongdoing. As unbelief, evil conduct, and injustice are the reasons for entering Hell, so are they the cause of Hell's existence and creation.

Some Prophetic traditions report that Hell exists under the Earth. The Earth's annual orbit outlines the extent of the Plain of Resurrection and Gathering after the Resurrection. This implies that Hell is under its orbit. It cannot be seen, because its fire gives off no light and is therefore invisible. Many beings exist within this orbit; however, we cannot see them because they emit no light. Just as the moon becomes invisible when hidden from the Sun's light, spheres and creatures that emit no light cannot be seen, even though they are in front of our eyes.

There are two Hells: one minor, the other major. The minor Hell is under the Earth or in its center. Geology teaches us heat increases by 1°C for every 33 meters toward the Earth's center. Thus, the temperature of the Earth's center is 200,000°C, given that the Earth's radius is 6,000 kilometers. This is in agreement with a Prophetic Tradition on this subject.

In this world and the intermediate one, the minor Hell fulfills many of the major Hell's functions. For example, it will be expanded into the major Hell in the other world. The Earth will empty its contents onto the Plain, built from its annual orbit, and will transfer the minor Hell to the major Hell.

---

67 ibid., "1st Letter."

Some leading figures of the Mu'tazili school of taught, mistakenly, that Hell would be created later. The truth is that Hell has not yet been fully expanded so as to contain all its future contents. Besides, the other world's stations are veiled from us. In order to see them, we would have to have eyes as penetrating as starlight, or to diminish the universe into small areas. The major Hell however, as implied in some Prophetic sayings, has a relation with this world. Intense summer heat, for instance, is described as "coming from Hell's heat."

Though we cannot see the major Hell or comprehend it with our mind's eye, we can glimpse something of its nature through the Divine Name the All-Wise.

The major Hell appears to have deputed some of its functions to the minor one. The sovereignty of an Omnipotent One of Majesty, a Wise One of Perfection, Who owns the absolute power of *Be! and it is*, has bound the moon to the Earth, and the Earth to the Sun with perfect wisdom and order. It set the Sun and its satellites moving, according to a theory, toward the sun of suns (the Vega star in the Lyra constellation) with a speed almost as great as that of the Earth's revolution around the Sun. He has made the stars as luminous evidence for His Mastership's sovereignty and His Power's greatness.

Such a power and wisdom can make the major Hell function as the source of the "heat and fire" of the stars, which look to the Heaven of the other world, and to illuminate them with the light of Paradise. He is able to make some sections of Hell a place of torment and a dungeon for people who deserve it. The Power of the Majestic, All-Wise Creator, Who makes a thumbnail-sized fruit-stone contain a tree, also can make the minor Hell encapsulate the major one until an appointed time.

In conclusion, Paradise and Hell are two fruits growing on the tip of a branch extending from the tree of creation far into eternity. They are two opposite outcomes of the chain of being. The places of these outcomes are on opposite ends of the chain: the degraded one on the lower end, and the luminous, sublime one on the upper.

Paradise and Hell are also two storerooms of the flow of worldly events and the world's spiritual products. One storeroom, which is being filled with evil products, is below; its opposite is above. They are also two pools, where two streams of beings are emptied. One carries the wicked and foul, while the other carries the good and pure. Paradise is where the Divine Favor and Mercy manifest themselves, and Hell is where God's wrath and awe are exhibited. The

Gracious, All-Merciful One, Who is All-Majestic and All-Omnipotent, manifests Himself (through His Names and Attributes) wherever He wishes.

ANSWERS TO QUESTIONS ABOUT PARADISE[68]

In the Name of God, the Merciful, the Compassionate. Give glad tidings to those who believe and do good deeds; for them are Gardens underneath which rivers flow; every time they are provided with fruit thereof, they say: "This is what we were provided with before," and it is given to them in resemblance. There are for them pure spouses, and they shall abide there forever. (2:25)

QUESTION: What does an individual's defective, changing, unstable, and pain-stricken body have to do with eternity and Paradise? The elevated pleasures of the spirit must be enough. Why should a bodily resurrection take place for corporal pleasures?

ANSWER: Despite its darkness and density in contrast to water, air, and light, soil is the means and source of all varieties of Divine art. Thus, it has some superiority to other elements. Despite the human selfhood's density, and on account of its comprehensiveness and provided that it is purified, it has some kind of superiority to other senses and faculties.

Likewise, the human body is a most comprehensive and rich mirror for manifesting the Divine Names. It can weigh and measure the contents of all Divine treasuries. For example, if the tongue's sense of taste was not the origin of as many measures as the varieties of food and drink, it could not experience each and recognize or measure them. Furthermore, the human body contains the instruments with which to experience and recognize most of the Divine Names' manifestations, as well as the faculties for experiencing the most various and infinitely different pleasures.

We can understand from the universe's conduct and human nature's comprehensiveness that its Maker wants to use the universe to display His Mercy's treasuries, to manifest all His Names, and to make us experience all His bounties. The world of eternal happiness, a mighty pool into which the flood of the universe flows, as well as a vast exhibition of the "loom" of the universe's products and the everlasting store of crops produced in the world's field, will resemble the universe to a certain degree. The All-Wise Maker, All-Compassionate Just One, will reward each bodily organ for its service and

---

68 Said Nursi, *The Words*, "28th Word."

particular type of worship with pleasures specific to it. To think otherwise would be contrary to His Wisdom, Justice, and Compassion.

QUESTION: A living body is always undergoing change and disintegration, and so cannot be eternal. Eating and drinking cause the individual to live, and sex allows the species to be perpetuated. As these are fundamental to worldly life, but are unneeded in the world of eternity, why have they been included among the greatest pleasures of Paradise?

ANSWER: Our bodies are doomed to decline and death because they are not balanced. From childhood until maturity, the body takes in more than it expends. Afterwards, its expenditures increase so much that the balance is eventually destroyed, causing the body to die.

In the world of eternity, the body's particles remain constant and immune to disintegration and re-formation; so the body is balanced. Like moving in perpetual cycles, a living body gains eternity through its constant operation for pleasure. Although eating, drinking, and sex between married couples arise from a need and perform a function, many excellent pleasures are ingrained in them as an immediate wage for the functions performed. They also are superior to other pleasures. Since eating and marriage lead to many wonderful and various pleasures, those pleasures will assume a most elevated form in Paradise, the realm of happiness and pleasure.

The pleasure of otherworldly wages for duties performed here, as well as the need felt for them here in the form of a pleasant and otherworldly appetite, will become an all-encompassing, living source of pleasure appropriate to Paradise and eternity.

> This life of the world is but a pastime and a game, but the home of the Hereafter, that is all living if they but knew. (29:64)

According to this verse, all lifeless and unconscious substances and objects here are living and conscious there. Like human beings and animals here, trees and stones there will understand and obey commands. If you tell a tree to bring you such-and-such a fruit, it will bring it. If you tell a stone to come, it will come. Since stones and trees will of necessity assume such an elevated form and preserve their bodily realities, eating, drinking, and marital relations also will assume higher forms there that are suitable to Paradise.

QUESTION: According to the hadith "A person is with whom he or she loves," friends will be together in Paradise. Therefore, a simple bedouin who feels a deep love for God's Messenger in one minute's companionship with him will be with him in Paradise. But how can a simple person's illumination and reward cause him or her to share the same place with God's Messenger, whose illumination and reward are limitless?

ANSWER: Consider the following comparison. In an extremely beautiful and splendid garden, a magnificent person prepares a vast banquet and richly adorned spectacle. Present are all the delicious foods that the sense of taste can experience, all beautiful things that please the sense of sight, all the wonders that amuse the faculty of imagination, and so on. Everything that would gratify and please all outer and inner senses is present.

Two friends go to the banquet and sit at a table within the same pavilion. One has only a limited ability to taste, weak eyesight, no sense of smell, and so cannot understand fully the wonderful arts or comprehend the marvels. This person benefits from the surroundings only within these limitations. But the other person, whose outer and inner senses, intellect, heart, and all faculties and feelings are developed to the utmost degree, perceives and experiences all the subtleties and beauties, marvels and fine things therein, and derives all varieties of pleasure from them.

This is the case with our own world, in which there can be an immeasurable distance between two friends who exist side by side. In Paradise, the abode of happiness and eternity, while friends are together it is only right that each receive his or her share from the Most Merciful One's table based on his or her ability to do so.

Besides, even though they are in different Paradises or on different "floors," they will be able to meet. The eight levels of Paradise are on top of each other, and the roof over all of them is the Supreme Throne of God. Suppose there are walled circles around a conical mountain, one within the other and one above the other, from its foot to the summit. Such an arrangement does not prevent anyone from seeing the sun. (Indeed, various Traditions indicate that Paradise's levels or floors are like this.)

QUESTION: Some Prophetic Traditions say: "Some of the people of Paradise will be given a place as large as the world, and hundreds of thousands of palaces will be granted to them." Why is this, and why does one person need all these things?

ANSWER: If people were only solid objects; creatures similar to plants, consisting of a stomach; or limited, heavy, simple, and transient corporal or animal bodies, they would not own or deserve so many palaces.

But people are such comprehensive miracles of Divine Power that even in this transient world and brief life, even if the whole world and all its wealth and pleasures were given to gratify some of their undeveloped senses and faculties, they would still desire more. But those with an infinite capacity in an eternal abode of happiness, who will knock on the door of infinite Mercy in the tongue of infinite need, will receive the Divine bounties described in hadiths. Consider the following comparison.

Each vineyard and garden in this town has a different owner. But each bird, sparrow, or honeybee in it, which possesses only a handful of grain, may say: "All of these vineyards and gardens are my places of recreation." Each may own the town and include it in its property, for the fact that others share in it does not limit its rule.

A true human being may say: "My Creator has made the world a home for me. The Sun is its chief lamp; the stars its electric lights. The Earth is my cradle spread with flowered carpets." Such a person thanks God. The fact that others share in this does not negate such a conclusion. On the contrary, they are more like decorations adorning his or her home.

If a person or even a bird in this world can claim ownership of such a vast area and receive such a vast bounty, how can it be considered unlikely that he or she will not own a property stretching for millions of miles in a broad and eternal abode of happiness?

Just as the Sun is present at the same moment in numerous mirrors, so a spiritually enlightened being can be in many places simultaneously. For example, Gabriel is present on 1,000 stars at the same moment he is at the Supreme Throne of God and in the Prophet's presence. Likewise, the Prophet, who can appear in countless places simultaneously in this world, will meet with most of the devoted, God-fearing members of his community in the Plain of Resurrection and Gathering at the same moment.

A group of saints known as *abdal* (substitutes) appear at the same moment in many places. Ordinary people sometimes do as much as a year's work in one minute in a dream, or travel as many places as they can in normal life in one year. Everyone gets in contact with and is concerned in many places at the same time in heart, in spirit, and in imagination. These are well-known and witnessed phenomena.

Paradise is a realm of light that is unrestricted, broad, and eternal. Its people, whose bodies will have the spirit's strength and lightness and the imagination's swiftness, will be in countless places at the same time, talk with countless friends, and receive pleasure in countless ways. This is fitting for the eternal Paradise and the infinite Mercy and, as reported by the Truthful Reporter, this is reality and the truth. Nevertheless, our human minds cannot grasp these vast truths.

QUESTIONS ON VARIOUS THEOLOGICAL MATTERS[69]

QUESTION: What will happen to those who were born and lived in non-Islamic countries?

ANSWER: Those who ask this question imply: "Since we believe in God and His Prophet, we will go to Paradise. But those who were born and live in non-Islamic countries do not benefit from the Divine Light and Guidance, and so will go to Hell."

There is no general statement or decree in Islam that those who live in non-Islamic countries will go to Hell. What is really said is this: Those who hear the Prophet's message and invitation and see the truth and light of Islam, but reject or ignore it, will go to Hell. To pretend to more mercy and compassion than the Compassion of God is the worst sort of impertinence. Whether those who hear the Divine Message live in Islamic countries or not is irrelevant; what matters is that they heed and obey it. Those who do not will go to Hell and suffer accordingly.

QUESTION: Is there a difference between those who consciously embrace unbelief and those who never heard of Islam? Will both go to Hell and suffer the same punishment?

ANSWER: This question has been dealt with at great length by Islamic theological scholars. The Ash'aris (followers of Imam al-Ash'ari in theological matters) held that one who has never heard the Name of God or been told anything about Him will not be punished. God rewards such people according to the good they did while alive, and they may enjoy the blessings of Paradise.

The Maturidis say something similar. They hold that if people discover the Creator through their reason, even though they do not know His Names or Attributes, they will be saved. But if they do not find the Creator through their reason, they will not be saved. They reason that, regardless of where someone lives, they can view natural phenomena (the "signs" of God) and can draw certain conclusions. Based on their observance of countless signs of the Owner, Creator, Sustainer, and Administrator of all things, they can observe and

---

69 Fethullah Gülen, *Questions and Answers about Faith*, The Fountain, Virginia: 2000.

acknowledge the Creator's absolute existence, power, and grace without know-ing His Names, Attributes, Books, and Messengers. Such people will not be punished.

Thus it is wrong to say that people who live in non-Islamic countries will go to Hell if they do not believe in God. Rather, we should remember what the leading Islamic theologians say and remain quiet.

Imam Ash'ari bases his ruling on: *We would never visit our wrath on any community until We had sent a Messenger to give warning* (17:15). So, some-one may not be punished for a wrong until a true Messenger has been sent to warn him or her.

According to the Maturidis, reason can discern good from evil. However, it would be wrong to go too far and say that reason can work out everything by itself. This is why God commands the good and forbids the evil, and never leaves the matter wholly to fallible human judgment and experience. He con-veys His commands and prohibitions through Messengers, and thus never leaves humanity in ignorance.

The Maturidi argument goes like this: Reason can work out that adultery and fornication are evil, because they cause genealogy and lineage to be inter-rupted and lost. As a result, such problems as dividing the deceased's estate arise. Reason can work out that theft is evil, because if it were normal no one could live in any degree of security. Reason can discover that drinking alcohol is evil, because it causes loss of consciousness, damages health, weakens resis-tance to many illnesses, and can even affect one's children. The same is true for what is good. One's reason recognizes justice, doing well by others, and so on as being good.

Reason can understand that faith in God is also good, for faith leads to satisfaction and inward contentment. Even in this world, we begin to sense the contentment we will have in Paradise. Reason can find its way to faith. Consider the following case: A bedouin came to the Prophet and explained how he found faith: "Camel droppings point to a camel's existence. Footprints on the sand tell of a traveler. The stars of Heaven, the Earth with its mountains and valleys, and the sea with its waves—don't they point to the Maker, All-Powerful, Knowing, Wise, and Caring?" He found faith by using his mind. Therefore, we must not underrate the role of reason and thinking in faith.

Setting out from this point, Imam al-Maturidi says that one may find the Creator through one's reason. There are many examples from pre-Islamic times. Among them is Waraqa ibn Nawfal, cousin of Khadija, the Prophet's first wife. Waraqa felt that a Prophet would come during his lifetime. When the first Revelation came to Muhammad, and he saw Gabriel fill the horizon and the heavens with his grandeur, he went home and, with his heart still quaking, told Khadija what he had seen and heard and then begged her to cover him. Khadija went to Waraqa for advice, and he confirmed the truth of Muhammad's mission and Revelations. Waraqa was among those who knew and had felt many of the already-fulfilled predicted signs of the Prophet's coming. Understanding that the idols were useless, he ignored them and, through his own judgment, believed in the existence of the One God.

Another such person was Zaid ibn 'Amr, the uncle of 'Umar ibn al-Khat-tab. A worshipper of the One God, he despised idols and told his people they were false and useless. He knew that a Prophet was coming soon, but did not live long enough to witness this event. He called his son Sa'id and 'Umar and other family members to his death-bed, and said: "The light of God is on the horizon. I believe it will emerge fully very soon. I already feel its signs over our heads. As soon as the Prophet comes, go and join him."

Whatever human beings make cannot be God or answer their needs, for they are themselves in need of human beings. How can such things be of any use to people? Through such simple reasoning, people can learn of their need to know the Master of the Earth and the Heavens. However, when people direct their minds and reason to Revelation, their need to know is met and the way to eternal bliss is opened.

In sum, those who saw or heard about the Prophet and the Qur'an, but for some reason refused to believe in them, will go to Hell. Those who remained in darkness through no fault of their own, and who had no chance to hear and learn about the Qur'an and the Prophet, may benefit from Divine Grace and not be blamed and punished for whatever wrongs they committed out of genuine ignorance.

QUESTION: What is reincarnation? Does it conform to the teachings of Islam?

ANSWER: Reincarnation refers to the transmigration of souls, the doctrine that after death the soul moves on to inhabit another body. This cycle continues as long as necessary. This doctrine is called reincarnation. It is not Islamic.

Belief in some form of reincarnation can be found in almost all societies, whether primitive or sophisticated. Variations exist according to local and regional differences in faith and popular culture. In the most materialistic societies, whose formal culture denies any spiritual life, there is almost a fashion for pseudo-religious belief that the souls of the dead wander about, sometimes taking physical form, and influence the living until they (the spirits) settle into their "new" bodies. Rather than going into such digressions, I will describe its main tenets and consider it from the Islamic viewpoint.

One argument for the antiquity of reincarnation is the "evidence" in ancient literature, such as tales of metamorphosis—for example, Ovid's colorful extravagances of that name, in which "deities" take on human and animal forms, human beings assume a diversity of different shapes, and so on. But these tales do not constitute a doctrine; the doctrine proper is that an individual spirit must pass through every "level" of creation, every species of life form, whether animate or inanimate, sentient or nonsentient.

Those who believe in reincarnation assert that souls emigrate from one level of earthly existence to another, from the bodies of human beings to animals, therefrom to plants and therefrom to inanimate objects. Spirits move up and down these levels of existence according to their actions. The emigration of a human soul to another human body is called "transmigration," and to an animal body "metamorphosis."

If we reflect upon this, we soon realize that the doctrine is an elaboration on the soul's immortality. Its kernel, the soul's immortality, is true; the rest is not. The doctrine also may have arisen from seeing similar physical and other traits between parents and offspring. In other words, the biological phenomenon of heredity, perfectly explained by genetics, is given a less intelligible, indeed irrational, explanation through reincarnation.

We can see a correlation between reincarnation and such similar false beliefs as *incarnation* (the doctrine that God takes on human form or has a body in human form) and *union* (the union of a human soul with God). This doctrine also may come from the belief of a universal soul taking on different forms, which gave rise to *monism*.

The doctrine is said to have emerged in the Nile basin and then spread as far a field as India, for example, and then westward to Greece. There, the eloquence of philosophers rationalized it (incredibly, it seems to us) into a source of consolation and hope for those who long for eternity. Among the major religions, the doctrine entered Judaism through Kabbalists, Christianity via Jewish thinkers, and finally into the ideas of some Sufis, despite the hard labors of Muslim theologians to refute such a distortion.

To support it, every apologist put forward some "evidence." For instance, the Kabbalists mention the transformation of Niobe (mentioned in the Old Testament) into a marble statue, and of Prophet Lot's wife into a pillar of salt.

Another argument for it is that it explains an animal's instinct and intelligence, and the splendors of the plant kingdom, as they once had human intelligence and vitality. This idea debases humanity and shames its proponents. It is really difficult to accept that such an assertion, even if made on the spur of the moment, could be made by intelligent people. Certainly there is a program and a predetermined destiny for plants and inanimate creations. But it is rather far-fetched to trace the harmony and order we see in the plant or mineral kingdoms to souls that formerly lived as or in human beings. Actually, plants and trees have a certain life, a plant-life, a direction of growth toward light and moisture. But this does not mean that this is the activity of a formerly human soul, or a soul on its way up the levels of creation.

Despite efforts to corroborate this, no one has ever received a message from a plant confirming that it contains a soul that once belonged to a human being, nor have we heard any person say that they were once souls in a plant or animal. Tabloids and other media spread tales of people recollecting "past lives," even recounting specific incidents. Where these claims are not totally absurd and ridiculous, their substance can easily be explained as recollections of what the individual has seen or read and then, knowingly or otherwise, elaborated and transformed as in any ordinary human fiction.

The fact that Niobe and Prophet Lot's wife were transformed into marble and salt statues, respectively, even if accepted literally, does not prove reincarnation. What we have here is a physical transformation having nothing to do with the soul's transmigration. Petrified bodies are not an arcane phenomenon: many such corpses have been found preserved by the absolute dryness of volcanic ashes. Consider the case of Pompeii, a city destroyed by a sudden volcanic eruption and unearthed from layers of ash only centuries later. Subsequent excavations revealed numerous Niobe-like petrified bodies.

In these ruins, and in the petrified faces and bodies of those so busy in their self-indulgent vices and so secure in their arrogance, we can, if we wish, read the signs of Divine wrath and punishment. Perhaps these figures had their way of life solidified in ash and thus preserved so that future generations might witness and take heed. To interpret them as evidence of reincarnation is simply untenable.

Belief in reincarnation in Egypt, India, and Greece developed out of a distorted version of belief in the Hereafter and from a longing for immortality of the soul. Neither Akhenaten's Egypt nor Pythagoras' Greece knew of reincarnation. Akhenaten believed that when human life ends, a different one starts in heaven. As soon as one dies, one's soul sets off on its journey to reach "the Greatest Court" in heaven. It goes so high that it reaches the presence of Osiris, and hopes to give an account of itself in words like these:

> I have not done falsehood against people. I have not impoverished my associates. I have done no wrong in the Place of Truth. I have not learned that which is not. I have done no evil. I have not made people labor daily in excess of what was due to be done for me ..

Those who can so speak join Osiris' congregation; those who cannot, whose evil deeds outweigh their good, are hurled into Hell and tortured by demons.

Such sound belief also is witnessed in epitaphs relating to Akhenaten's religion as follows:

> What You have done is too much, and our eyes cannot perceive most of them. O One, Only God! No one possesses such might as You have. It is You who have created this universe as You wish and You alone. It is You who decree the world suitable for human beings, for all animals, whether big or small, whether they walk on the Earth on their legs or they fly up in the sky on their wings. And it is You alone who sustain and nourish them. Thanks to You, all beauties come into existence. All eyes see You by means of those. Verily, my heart belongs to You (You are in my heart).[70]

The ideas quoted verbatim above were believed as truth some 4,000 years ago in Egypt.

Likewise, in ancient Greece, belief in the Resurrection and the soul's immortality were quite sound. The great philosopher Pythagoras, for example, believed that the soul, on leaving the body, acquires its own kind of life. In fact, any soul has this kind of life even before it quits the Earth. It is commissioned with some responsibilities on Earth. If it commits any evil, it will be punished, thrown into Hell, and tormented by demons; if it does good, it will be given a high rank and blessed with a happy life.

---

70 J. H. Breasted, *A History of Egypt*, Simon Publications, 2001.

Allowing for changes that might have been made in his views over time, we can still see that there are fundamental similarities with the Islamic creed of the Resurrection. Plato's account is not so different either. In his famous *Republic,* he says that when the soul leaves the body, it forgets the material (corporeal) life totally and ascends to an appropriate spiritual realm saturated with wisdom and immortality. There, it is free from all scarcity, deficiency, error, fear, and from the passion and love that afflicted it on Earth. Being free of all evil consequences of human nature, it is blessed with eternal bliss.

In essence, all variations of the doctrine of reincarnation are distorted versions of a sound belief: the soul's immortality and the intrinsic human desire for eternity. The human soul has an existence that is different from, and even independent of, the body. For example, St. Thomas Aquinas, one of the most famous Christian theologians and philosophers, writes that the key concept of humanity is that the soul and body are united in an apt composite.[71] He adds that animal souls develop with animal bodies, whereas human souls are specially created at some time during early development.

Over time, borrowings from or interactions with certain ancient beliefs enabled such false doctrines to filter into sound beliefs. One cannot miss the relation between reincarnation and the deification of Jesus, which is related to such false doctrines as *union* and *incarnation.*

In a comparable way, no doubt through mistaken (whether deliberate or not) translations from the original language and later distortions, ancient Egyptian, Indian, and Greek religions became unrecognizable. The doctrine of reincarnation may well be one such alteration from an originally sound conception of the soul's immortality and its return to the Divine Judgment.

After reincarnation was inscribed into the beliefs of the ancient Egyptians, it became a central theme of songs and legends throughout the Nile region. Elaborated further with the eloquent expressions of Greek philosophers, it became, with the expansion of Greek influence, a widespread phenomenon.

Hindus consider matter the lowest manifestation of Brahman, and deem the convergence of body and soul as demeaning to the soul, a decline into evil. Death is believed to be salvation, a separation from human defect and a possible chance to achieve an ecstatic union with the truth. Hindus are polytheistic.

One of their gods is Krishna, who is believed to have come in a human figure to eradicate evil. Another god is Vishnu, who can penetrate the human

---

71 *Summa Theologica*, Part I, Question 90, Art. 3, 4.

body. Hindus believe that Vishnu has descended into this world nine times in different shapes (human, animal, or flower). He is expected to descend for the tenth time. Since they believe that Vishnu will next come to this world in the shape of an animal, killing any animal, except during war, is absolutely prohibited. Devout Hindus are usually vegetarians.

According to the *Vedanta*, an important Hindu religious text, the soul is a part of Brahman that will never be free of suffering and distress until it returns to its origin. The soul achieves gnosis by isolating itself from the ego and all wickedness pertaining to the ego, and by running toward Brahman, just as a river flows to a sea. When the soul reaches and unites with Brahman, it acquires absolute peace, tranquility, and stillness. This doctrine also is found in the Buddhist idea of Nirvana. There is an abatement of active seeking, and a passivity of soul in the latter, whereas the soul is dynamic in Hinduism.

Some Jewish sects adopted reincarnation. After refusing belief in the Resurrection and Judgment, these people, who can be inordinately covetous of life yet remain fascinated by the soul's immortality, could do little else than accept reincarnation. Later, the Kabbalists transferred it to the Church of Alexandria through certain regional monastic orders. The doctrine, which has had a negligible effect on Islam, was introduced to Muslims by the Gulat al-Shi'a (an extremist Shi'a faction).

All ancient, new, and contemporary versions of reincarnation have one root characteristic: belief in incarnation. There is a shared failure of intellect to grasp and accept the Absolute Transcendence of God. Corrupted by this failure, people believe that the Divine mixes with the human, and that the human will (or can) mix with the Divine. This error is, except for Islam which has retained its strict purity of belief, all but universal.

The central figure in each distorted belief is an incarnation or reincarnation: Aten in Atenism, Brahman in Hinduism, Ezra (Uzair) in Judaism, Jesus in Christianity, and 'Ali in the Gulat al-Shi'a faction who, if they exist at all within Islam, must be seen as on its very outermost fringes. Allegations that some Sufi writings and utterances support reincarnation are either plainly malicious or the result of an absurdly literal understanding of their highly symbolic and esoteric discourse. Islamic scholars and theologians, certainly among the 90 percent of Sunnis, reject reincarnation as contrary to Islam.

This is true of scholars in every field—jurisprudence, theology, Qur'anic commentary, or hadith commentary. Their reason: the absolute centrality in Islam that each individual lives and dies according to his or her own destiny, carries his or her own load, will be resurrected and called individually to answer for his or her intentions and actions and their consequences, and will be judged individually by God (with perfect justice) according to the same criteria.

We now present the cardinal reasons why Islam rejects reincarnation. Belief in Islam requires belief in the Resurrection and Judgment, when justice is meted out to each individual soul according to that individual's record in life. If the individual soul passes into different lives, in which form or personality will it be resurrected, commanded to give account, and rewarded or punished?

This world is created to test and try the soul so that it may benefit thereby. One focus of the test is belief in the Unseen. According to reincarnation, those who live a bad life pass into a lower form of life (animal, tree, etc.) after death. After undergoing cycles of suffering, their lives will end in some way, which means the end of the cycles of reincarnation. Therefore, by its very nature, reincarnation is not a final end and does not contradict the world's final destruction and the Supreme Judgment.

To get around this, believers in this doctrine have a doctrine of forgetfulness—the soul "forgets" its past existence. In that case, for all practical purposes, having had (or not having had) a past existence is of no consequence. Plainly, the doctrine contradicts itself and has no bearing on the "current" life except to make the individual accept his or her condition without actively striving for salvation.

If each individual is supposed to go through a painful cycle of transmigration to acquire eternal bliss, then God's promise to punish the wicked and the sinful and to reward the good and the righteous, has no meaning for the individual life. This is unacceptable for Providence, for God is neither vain nor futile in His actions.

The Qur'an and other Divine Books state that sins will be forgiven (if truly repented). This proves how unnecessary and cumbersome a doctrine reincarnation is. How much better do the concepts of mercy and forgiveness befit God, the Beneficent, Merciful Creator.

In Islam, there is no sin that God will not forgive, as He wills. God, the All-Mighty, reveals and promises in the Qur'an that He will forgive those who repent and sincerely intend to abandon such behavior. In this respect, God does not see how great or little your sins are, nor how late your penitence is. This may mean that a sinner who disobeys and rebels against God throughout his or her life can be forgiven by a single act of true repentance, done with absolute sincerity and a profound understanding of servanthood and dependence on God.

Long and tiresome cycles of rebirth are contrary to the mercy, favor, and grace of God, the All-Compassionate. If He wills, He takes ordinary, worthless, inferior things and turns them into what is purest, best, and beyond price. His blessings and munificence are infinite.

Many followers of the Prophets led wicked lives but then reformed within an incredibly short time and became revered models of virtue for later generations. After meeting the Prophets and embracing the Divine Message, some surpassed previous followers and came to be even more revered. This indicates that, by the favor of God, one can rise easily and quickly to the summit, even if one seemed to be destined for the pit. It shows, again, how *unnecessary* the doctrine of souls "graduating" into higher levels of being is. Indeed, the doctrine may have the effect of lessening incentives to moral effort.

To believe that God, the All-Mighty, has created a soul for each individual is part of belief in His Omnipotence. To believe that a limited number of souls migrate from body to body argues the illogical proposition that the Omnipotent is not Omnipotent. The sheer abundance of life, its infinite variety, its refusal of mere repetition of form, is everywhere evident: God is indeed All-Mighty.

There are approximately 6 or 6.5 billion people in the world. In recent times, we have learned how to prove that each individual is absolutely unique—an idea urged by many verses of the Qur'an—by looking at fingerprints or genetic codes. These facts are so reliable that they are used in forensic science to identify criminals. Another example is the observation, over 30 years, of millions of pictures of snowflakes—not one of which is ever exactly like any other. We cannot even imagine how many snowflakes fall in one season on one mountainside, let alone all that have ever fallen. How foolish to imply, then, that the Omnipotent could not create an infinite number of individual souls and supply each with a unique body.

Could not a few million people out of the billions now living have at least some marks, signs, evidence, or something convincing to tell of their memories, adventures, and experiences in different forms and bodies? Has there not been an accumulation of knowledge, experience, and culture in some of those reincarnated beings or those who have completed their cycles? If this happened in only one out of a million people, should we not expect to see a great number of people now living with extraordinary virtue and competence? Should we not have met a few of them even in our own countries? If so, where are they?

Even if some in non-Muslim countries people claim to remember past lives, why do so few people in the Muslim world make such claims?

If reincarnation educates souls so that they become pure enough to attain salvation, would it not be logical for those returning to the world to draw lessons from their previous lives and thus remember their former sins and shortcomings? Is there a single example that demonstrates this?

When a body reaches an age (say of 3 or 4), a measure of physical maturity, should we not expect the soul to emerge with all that it has acquired and achieved in its former lives? Should we not expect prodigies? There have been quite a few prodigies in recorded history, but their special gifts need not be the result of former lives. Such cases can be explained equally well as a special combination of genetic characteristics occurring in a particular time and place, which is attributable to Divine Grace and Favor. Added to this is the individual's own supreme effort to understand his or her own gift in the tradition and context in which it is given.

No faculty unique to human beings has ever been found in any non-human entity, whether animate or inanimate. But we should expect such a discovery if there were any truth in reincarnation. If a lower form of life is, so to speak, the consequence (punishment) for particular evil deeds in a previous life, then presumably the good in that life (outweighed by the evil) must be carried forward.

In other words, some part of the individual's previous life should be retained in the next life. In this case, we would expect the boundaries of particular forms to be frequently burst open—with, for example, plants suddenly showing animal-like properties. But, by the Mercy of God, zoology and botany have not, for all their many welcome advances in recent years, discovered any such monsters.

If being a human or an animal is the consequence of one's deeds in a former life, which existed first: human or animal, the higher or the lower? Advocates of reincarnation cannot decide or agree on any form for the first creature, for every generation implies a preceding generation in order that the succeeding generation may be considered as the consequence of the former. And if generation is an evil, as some who believe in reincarnation also believe, why did the whole thing start? Why did life begin at all? Plainly, the doctrine leads again and again to absurdity.

SELECTED BIBLIOGRAPHY

Islamic Perspectives on Science, "What a Falling Stone Means" by Salih Adem, "Worldwide Corruption by Scientific Materialism" by Dr. Suat Yildirim, Kaynak, Izmir: 1998.

Fethullah Gülen, *The Essentials of the Islamic Faith*, The Light, Inc., New Jersey: 2005.

_____. Fethullah Gülen, *Questions and Answers about Faith*, The Fountain, Virginia: 2000.

Said Nursi, *The Words*, The Light, Inc., New Jersey: 2005.

_____. Said Nursi, *The Letters*, Truestar, London: 1995.

_____. Said Nursi, *The Rays Collection*, Sozler Publications, Istanbul: 2002.

Dr. Collin Turner, "Risale-i Nur, A Revolution of Belief." Paper offered to a conference held about Bediüzzaman Said Nursi in Istanbul in 1993.